FAVOURITE FOOD MEMORIES

grub

jane lawson

acknowledgments

To Kay Scarlett — thank you so very much for always sharing the vision and for your relentless energy and enthusiasm.
To Juliet Rogers and all the wonderful staff at Murdoch Books — thank you all, once again, for making this happen.
To Rhiain Hull — thrown in at the deep end, you have been amazingly patient with me through the whole 'broken neck' episode — you are a true gem. Thanks for everything!
To Katri Hilden — great working with you again, even if it was at the 11th hour! Thanks for your patience with the long-distance factor and for always being so damn pleasant! Thanks also to Paul McNally.
To Vivien Valk and Lauren Camilleri — thanks for 'getting it' and working so hard to bring it together.
To uber photographer Steve Brown, the talented stylists Justine Osborne and Vanessa Austin, the ever fabulous Rossy Dobson, Grace Campbell and Wendy Quisumbing — thank you all so very much for adding colour and movement!
To Vicky Harris and Christine Osmond — thanks for all your help chicks!
Much love and thanks to my dear family and friends for their endless support and appreciation of good food. A special thanks to mum, Ness and family, and Kim for looking after me so well during my extended stint on the lounge-room floor.
And finally, cheers to our ancestors for passing stuff down!

For my Nana Doris — whose final chapter came to a close just prior to my finishing this book. Travel well, give my love to Dad and Harry and make sure you hide the Xmas cake well.

Published in 2007 by Murdoch Books Pty Limited
www.murdochbooks.com.au

Murdoch Books Australia
Pier 8/9
23 Hickson Road
Millers Point NSW 2000
Phone: +61 (0) 2 8220 2000
Fax: +61 (0) 2 8220 2558

Murdoch Books UK Limited
Erico House
6th Floor
93–99 Upper Richmond Road
Putney, London SW15 2TG
Phone: +44 (0) 20 8785 5995
Fax: +44 (0) 20 8785 5985

Chief Executive: Juliet Rogers
Publishing Director: Kay Scarlett

Design Concept, Art Direction and Design: Lauren Camilleri
Project Manager: Rhiain Hull
Editor: Katri Hilden
Production: Maiya Levitch
Photographer: Steve Brown
Stylists: Justine Osborne front cover and all pages except 19, 42, 72–3, 96–7, 100, 108–9, 113, 118, 171, 172, 195, 208–9; Vanessa Austin back cover and pages 19, 42, 72–3, 96–7, 100, 108–9, 113, 118, 171, 172, 195, 208–9.
Food Preparation: Grace Campbell, Ross Dobson, Wendy Quisumbing

National Library of Australia Cataloguing-in-Publication Data
Lawson, Jane. Grub. Includes index.
ISBN 978 1 74045 873 3. ISBN 1 74045 873 7.
1. Cookery. 1. Title. 641.5

A catalogue record for this book is available from the British Library.

Printed by Midas Printing (Asia) Ltd in 2007. PRINTED IN CHINA.
CONVERSION GUIDE: You may find cooking times vary depending on the oven you are using. For fan-forced ovens, as a general rule, set the oven temperature to 20°C (35°F) lower than indicated in the recipe. We have used 20 ml (4 teaspoon) tablespoon measures. If you are using a 15 ml (3 teaspoon) tablespoon, for most recipes the difference will not be noticeable. However, for recipes using baking powder, gelatine, bicarbonate of soda (baking soda), small amounts of flour and cornflour (cornstarch), add an extra teaspoon for each tablespoon specified.

FAVOURITE FOOD MEMORIES

grub

jane lawson

MURDOCH BOOKS

GRUB//

a slang/colloquial term for food. The origins of the word 'grub' are rather hazy. However, there is suggestion that it hails from seventeenth-century England, based on the notion that 'to grub' means 'to dig' — which may sound a little strange, but if you consider that many foods are indeed 'dug up' from the land, or perhaps if you have ever mouthed the words 'let's eat whatever we can dig up', the term may begin to make sense...

introduction

Like many people, when it comes to food, instead of 'digging up' the basics I spend too much time searching out the new and exotic — so much so that the dishes that we, our parents, and grandparents before them grew up on have sadly been cast aside or ignored, tagged as boring or old fashioned. Sure, our palates and waistlines have become a little more discerning, so naturally some foods may have lost their appeal, but on this quest for the newest foodie kick have we forgotten how nurturing and comforting many of these centuries-old and well-proven recipes can be? I had. Guilty as charged!

In an effort to get in touch with a little of our heritage in the best way I know how, this collection of very personal recipes was born. What an immense joy it was to write this book! I am so very privileged to have had the opportunity to cook and, best of all, eat all my old favourites again — plus a few new ones — reliving so many special foodie memories from my childhood. Why had it taken me so long to realize how wonderful these dishes were and still are? And it isn't just the food, it's the emotions attached to it — the steaming bowl of tomato soup your mum administered while you were wrapped in a crocheted blanket with a dose of the sniffles, the lemon meringue pie that used to cool on the windowsill in the spring breeze, the warm date loaf with a smear of butter after school, tucking into a rich and hearty Irish stew on a winter's evening, or the aroma of a juicy steak sizzling on the barbecue on a summer's day while you played under the sprinkler.

For me, this book is a reference tool, a home to all those traditional or inherited family recipes you can never find, a replacement of smudged, dog-eared newspaper clippings or hand-scribbled notes you didn't quite get round to typing up. It contains the very best versions of all our favourites, mostly traditional — well at least the way I remember them — and some with a contemporary twist. Some more 'modern' recipes borrow flavours from Asia, whose fragrant ingredients have become so popular in the Western world.

I humbly invite you to share in my treasured selection of recipes and hope you enjoy revisiting many cherished moments while you treat your tastebuds, just as I did. However, I eagerly encourage you to keep a record of your own mum's dinner 'special', your nanna's prize-winning cake recipe or your dad's hot tips for the barbecue. And don't forget to pass them on to your family and friends — keep the joy alive for generations to come!

chapter one *in the MORNING

LIVING ON A BIG ISLAND WITH AN AMAZING SHORELINE AND BEAUTIFUL COUNTRYSIDE, IT IS LITTLE WONDER I LIKE TO START THE DAY WITH A DELICIOUS, NUTRITIOUS AND OCCASIONALLY DECADENT BREAKFAST WHILE TAKING IN THE VIEW. I AM LUCKY ENOUGH TO LIVE NEAR THE BEACH, AND BREAKFAST IS MORE OFTEN THAN NOT BUSIER THAN LUNCH IN MANY OF THE LOCAL CAFÉS. ON SUNDAY MORNINGS YOU NEED TO BE EARLY IF YOU WANT A SEAT, BUT FORTUNATELY BREAKFAST IS SERVED WAY INTO THE AFTERNOON FOR LATE RISERS. DELICIOUS SEASONAL FRUITS AND LIGHTER OFFERINGS ARE THE MOST OBVIOUS PICKS NEAR THE SEASIDE. FURTHER INLAND, WHETHER WORKING IN THE COUNTRY OR INHALING CRISP MOUNTAIN AIR, APPETITES CRAVE MORE SUBSTANTIAL FARE — AND PLENTY OF IT FOR THOSE WORKING THE LAND.

* bacon & egg rolls with rocket & home-made barbecue sauce * corn & prawn jaffles * mangoes, strawberries & vanilla rosewater yoghurt * macadamia, fig & wattleseed muesli * aromatic stewed tomatoes with eggs * porridge with granny smith compote * pikelets with mulberry compote & cinnamon butter * banana bread with brown sugar butter * spicy baked beans * scrambled eggs with asparagus & salmon roe * welsh rarebit * garlic mushrooms & avocado on damper * bubble & squeak patties with lamb cutlets * crumpets with ginger mascarpone, nectarines & golden syrup * parmesan omelette with creamed spinach & roasted cherry tomatoes * coconut couscous with fruit in ginger mint syrup

✳ *Some mornings call for a savoury breakfast that's simple yet substantial, and nothing fits the bill better than the humble bacon and egg roll — the vital ingredient of course being a sweetly spicy, smoky barbecue sauce. Perfect for breakfast 'on the go', but don't forget the napkins for sticky fingers...*

bacon & egg rolls
with rocket & home-made barbecue sauce

BARBECUE SAUCE

1 tablespoon olive oil

1/2 small brown onion, chopped

1 1/2 tablespoons tomato paste (concentrated purée)

1 tablespoon golden syrup (if unavailable, substitute with 2 teaspoons each honey & dark corn syrup)

1 1/2 tablespoons worcestershire sauce

pinch of cayenne pepper

1/4 teaspoon smoked sweet paprika

1 1/2 teaspoons mustard powder

6 long, thin slices of good-quality bacon

olive oil, for pan-frying

4 large eggs, at room temperature

2 large handfuls of baby rocket (arugula) leaves or baby English spinach

4 soft white bread rolls, split & buttered

serves 4

To make the barbecue sauce, heat the olive oil in a small saucepan over medium–high heat. Add the onion and sauté for 5 minutes, or until lightly golden. Stir in the tomato paste and cook for a few seconds, then add the golden syrup, worcestershire sauce, cayenne pepper, paprika, mustard powder and 80 ml (2 1/2 fl oz/ 1/3 cup) water. Bring to the boil, then reduce the heat and simmer, stirring occasionally, for 8 minutes, or until thickened. Season to taste and set aside.

Cut the bacon into half-lengths. Brush a large frying pan with a little olive oil and place over high heat. Add the bacon and cook, turning occasionally, for 4–5 minutes, or until cooked to your liking.

When the bacon is almost ready, heat a little more olive oil in a large, heavy-based frying pan over medium–high heat and carefully crack the eggs into the pan, keeping them well spaced so they don't run into each other (use egg rings if you prefer). Fry the eggs until cooked to your liking — if you like your yolks runny like I do, especially when served in a roll, don't flip the egg, just cook it without turning for 2–3 minutes, or until the white is fully set and the yolk is still a little wobbly.

Put some baby salad leaves on the bottom half of each bread roll and top each one with three pieces of bacon, an egg and a dollop of the barbecue sauce. Top with the bread roll lids and serve immediately. This one is best eaten with your hands!

Before the electric sandwich maker there was ... the jaffle iron! Traditionally used in Australian campfire cooking to toast sandwiches over an open flame, the jaffle iron (also called a pie iron in the US) was made of two circular cast-iron moulds with long handles that clipped together around two slices of bread to seal in a filling. It sat over the open fire and is still popular with campfire cooks today. The jaffle iron could also be used at home on the stove hotplate and simply needed to be turned halfway through cooking. In our house the filling was usually cheese and tomato or baked beans, but sometimes for a snack or dessert we would make 'apple pies' using some thinly sliced apple, sugar and cinnamon — I can still taste them. This modern version contains another favourite — creamed corn — but has been dressed up by the addition of prawns, chilli, fresh coriander and spring onion. A savoury breakfast treat that also doubles as a wonderful afternoon or supper snack.

❈ corn & prawn jaffles

310 g (11 oz) tin creamed corn
1½ spring onions (scallions), chopped
12 cooked prawns (shrimp), peeled,
    deveined & chopped
½ long red chilli, seeded & finely chopped
½ teaspoon finely grated fresh ginger
1 handful of coriander (cilantro), chopped
white pepper, for seasoning
softened butter, for spreading
8 slices of white or wholemeal (whole-wheat) bread

serves 4

Preheat a toasted-sandwich maker, or preheat a hotplate to medium–high if using an old-fashioned jaffle iron.

Combine the corn, spring onion, prawn, chilli, ginger and coriander and season well with salt and a little white pepper.

Butter all the bread slices on one side. Place a quarter of the corn and prawn mixture on the unbuttered sides of four bread slices. Top each with another slice of bread, buttered side up. Place in the heated sandwich maker and cook for 4–5 minutes or until golden all over, or place in the jaffle iron and cook for 2–3 minutes on each side, or until golden all over. Serve immediately.

VARIATIONS: Naturally you can use your favourite toasted-sandwich fillings in a jaffle, but you can also be quite adventurous by using fancy bread, yummy leftovers, a variety of cheeses and cold meats, roast vegetables, fresh herbs, chutneys and relishes — you can even carefully crack an egg inside. Sweet jaffles are also delicious and perfect for an easy dessert.

mangoes, strawberries & vanilla rosewater yoghurt

Nothing puts a smile on my face more quickly on a summer's morning than tucking into this light breakfast 'trifle' after a brisk walk along the beach. Luscious fruits and the creamiest of yoghurt with the crunch of toasted almonds — heaven!

2 large ripe mangoes
250 g (9 oz/1⅔ cups) ripe strawberries, hulled
500 g (1 lb 2 oz/2 cups) thick & creamy plain
  yoghurt
1 teaspoon natural vanilla extract
2 teaspoons rosewater
30 g (1 oz/⅓ cup) flaked almonds, toasted
ground cinnamon, for sprinkling, optional

serves 4

Peel the mangoes and dice the flesh. Slice the strawberries. Mix together the yoghurt, vanilla extract and rosewater.

Divide the mango among four short, wide glasses or small glass bowls. Add a dollop of the yoghurt. Scatter the strawberries over the top, then dollop with the remaining yoghurt and garnish with the flaked almonds. Sprinkle with cinnamon if desired.

Refrigerate until ready to serve.

macadamia, fig & wattleseed muesli

300 g (10½ oz/3 cups) rolled (porridge) oats
160 g (5¾ oz/1 cup) unsalted macadamia nuts or
    blanched almonds, roughly chopped
30 g (1 oz/½ cup) shredded coconut
50 g (1¾ oz/⅓ cup) sesame seeds
115 g (4 oz/⅓ cup) golden syrup (if unavailable,
    substitute with half honey & half dark corn syrup)
40 g (1½ oz) unsalted butter
½ teaspoon natural vanilla extract
¼ teaspoon ground ginger
95 g (3¼ oz/½ cup) chopped dried figs
1½ teaspoons ground toasted wattleseed, optional

makes 6–8 servings

Preheat the oven to 170°C (325°F/Gas 3). Combine the rolled oats, macadamia nuts, coconut and sesame seeds and spread out in a large roasting tin. Place in the heated oven for about 5 minutes.

Meanwhile, gently heat the golden syrup, butter, vanilla and ground ginger in a small saucepan until runny. Pour the syrup mixture over the rolled oat mixture and mix thoroughly to coat well. Bake for 16–18 minutes, stirring and shaking the roasting tin regularly until the muesli is toasted. Remove from the oven and allow to cool completely, then stir through the figs and the wattleseed, if using.

Keep in an airtight container for up to 1 month. Serve with milk, or sprinkled over some creamy yoghurt.

VARIATION: Try adding some chopped dates in place of the figs.

You may never buy muesli again once you realize how simple and satisfying it is to make it yourself. Invented in Switzerland in 1900, this breakfast staple has found a home on many distant shores. Here it takes on a distinctly Australian 'bush tucker' feel with the addition of macadamia nuts, golden syrup and wattleseed, a native ingredient with a slight coffee flavour. Wattleseed adds an extra hint of toastiness, but if you can't find it, simply leave it out.

aromatic stewed tomatoes with eggs

60 ml (2 fl oz/¼ cup) olive oil

30 g (1 oz) butter, plus extra, for spreading

1 red onion, finely sliced

2 garlic cloves, crushed

1 small red chilli, seeded & finely chopped, optional

1½ teaspoons sweet paprika

½ red capsicum (pepper), diced

3 x 400 g (14 oz) tins chopped roma (plum) tomatoes

¼ teaspoon finely grated lemon zest

1 handful of basil leaves, shredded

1 handful of flat-leaf (Italian) parsley, shredded

60 ml (2 fl oz/¼ cup) balsamic vinegar

1 teaspoon soft brown sugar

8 small eggs

4 slices of pide (Turkish/flat) bread, each about
   10 cm (4 inches) wide

serves 4

Put the olive oil and butter in a very large, deep frying pan over medium–high heat. Add the onion and sauté for 4 minutes, or until lightly golden. Add the garlic, chilli and paprika and cook for 1 minute, or until fragrant. Add the capsicum, chopped tomatoes, lemon zest, half the basil and parsley, the vinegar, sugar, 1 teaspoon salt and 250 ml (9 fl oz/1 cup) water. Bring to the boil, then reduce the heat and simmer for 20 minutes, or until thickened slightly. Season to taste.

Carefully crack the eggs on top of the tomato mixture, spacing them a little apart. Cover with a lid and cook for 10–12 minutes, or until the whites of the eggs are set and the yolks are cooked to your liking. (You may also poach or fry the eggs separately if your pan isn't large enough to cook all the eggs at once. Or you could divide the tomato mixture between two frying pans and cook four eggs in each pan — the cooking time will be shorter.)

Meanwhile, split each piece of bread in half and place cut side up under a hot grill (broiler) until lightly golden. Spread each slice with a little butter, then carefully lift one egg with some of the tomato mixture onto each toasted bread slice. Sprinkle with the remaining herbs and serve immediately, allowing two eggs per person.

Old-fashioned stewed tomatoes make a delicious side dish or a saucy base to more elaborate recipes, but importantly stewing has always been a good method of preserving this versatile fruit during a seasonal glut. My mum loves stewed tomatoes on toast and wishes cafés would serve them up instead of the standard grilled tomato halves, which are often too firm and sometimes still cold in the middle. I've injected a little Spanish flavour by adding a hint of paprika, garlic and chilli — the method also happens to be similar to 'huevos flamencos', a Spanish egg and tomato dish. I love the fact that you cook the eggs in the tomato mixture — one less pan to wash, which is always a drawcard for me!

Winter mornings call for something warming and sustaining to see you through the day. Granny smiths, a tart yet sweet apple variety named after the woman who is credited with first producing the attractive bright-green fruit, disintegrate when cooked for a long time, making a lush, caramelly addition to creamy, wholesome porridge. This recipe makes a little more apple compote than you need, but with good reason — it is fabulous stirred through yoghurt, or dolloped onto crumpets or freshly baked scones.

*porridge
with granny smith compote

GRANNY SMITH COMPOTE

115 g (4 oz/½ cup) caster (superfine) sugar
45 g (1¾ oz/¼ cup) soft brown sugar
1 cinnamon stick
½ vanilla bean, split lengthways
6 cm (2½ inch) strip of lemon zest
3 granny smith apples, peeled, cored & chopped

150 g (5½ oz/1½ cups) rolled (porridge) oats
560 ml (19¼ fl oz/2¼ cups) milk
35 g (1¼ oz/⅓ cup) toasted walnuts, chopped
pouring (whipping) cream or milk, to serve

serves 4–6

To make the granny smith compote, put the caster sugar and brown sugar in a saucepan with the cinnamon stick, vanilla bean, lemon zest and 625 ml (21½ fl oz/2½ cups) water. Stir over high heat until the sugar has dissolved. Bring to the boil, then add the apple and bring to the boil again. Reduce the heat to very low and allow to slowly simmer for about 2 hours, stirring regularly to ensure the mixture doesn't stick to the pan. The mixture should become caramel-coloured, thick and pulpy — almost puréed. Remove the cinnamon, vanilla and lemon zest.

Meanwhile, make the porridge. Put the rolled oats, milk, a pinch of salt and 375 ml (13 fl oz/1½ cups) water in a saucepan and stir over medium–high heat until the mixture just comes to the boil. Reduce the heat to a simmer and stir regularly for 4–5 minutes, or until the porridge has thickened and the oats are very tender.

Serve the porridge in bowls, dolloped with the apple compote and sprinkled with chopped walnuts. Serve the cream or milk in a small jug on the side for pouring over.

Pikelets are more commonly enjoyed as an afternoon treat, but if Americans can eat pancakes for breakfast, what's to stop anyone indulging in a little stack of humble pikelets? (They are a simple pancake, after all!) The word 'pikelet' stems from the Welsh, but in parts of the UK the pikelet is also known as a drop scone as it is dropped onto the griddle or pan to cook.

pikelets with mulberry compote & cinnamon butter

MULBERRY COMPOTE

55 g (2 oz/¼ cup) caster (superfine) sugar
2 teaspoons lemon juice
300 g (10½ oz) mulberries (blackberries can be substituted)
¼ teaspoon natural vanilla extract

CINNAMON BUTTER

100 g (3½ oz) unsalted butter, diced
2 teaspoons ground cinnamon
30 g (1 oz/¼ cup) icing (confectioners') sugar

PIKELETS

185 g (6½ oz/1½ cups) self-raising flour
1½ tablespoons caster (superfine) sugar
2 large eggs
330 ml (11¼ fl oz/1⅓ cups) milk
melted butter, for pan-frying

makes 36 pikelets

To make the mulberry compote, put the sugar, lemon juice and 2 tablespoons water in a frying pan over high heat. Stir until the sugar has dissolved, then bring to the boil. Cook for 2 minutes, or until the mixture is sticky and bubbling and the edges are just starting to turn pale golden. Add the mulberries and stir gently. Reduce the heat to low and cook, stirring occasionally, for 2–3 minutes, or until the berries have softened slightly. Remove the berries with a slotted spoon and set aside. Increase the heat and bring the syrup to the boil. Add the vanilla and cook for 2 minutes, or until thick and glazy. Add the berries again and toss to coat. Remove from the heat and cover to keep warm. Makes about 1¼ cups.

Meanwhile, make the cinnamon butter by beating the butter, cinnamon and icing sugar together until pale and creamy. Set aside while you cook the pikelets. If your kitchen is warm, you might like to refrigerate the butter, then bring it out and beat again just before serving.

To make the pikelets, sift the flour, sugar and a pinch of salt into a bowl and make a well in the centre. Lightly whisk the eggs and milk together, then pour into the well. Whisk to a smooth batter and allow to rest for 15 minutes.

Heat a large, non-stick frying pan over medium heat and brush with a little melted butter. Drop tablespoons of the batter into the pan, leaving plenty of room for spreading. Cook for 40 seconds, or until bubbles appear on the surface and the underside is golden, then flip and cook for a further 30 seconds. Remove and keep warm while cooking the remaining batter. (The mixture makes about 38 pikelets, but the first couple are testers and are usually less attractive, so eat them while no-one is looking!)

Serve the pikelets in stacks, topped with a dollop of the cinnamon butter, with the mulberry compote in a small dish on the side for spooning over.

banana bread
with brown sugar butter

150 g (5^1/$_2$ oz) unsalted butter, chopped &
   slightly softened
115 g (4 oz/^{1}/$_2$ cup) caster (superfine) sugar
45 g (1^3/$_4$ oz/^{1}/$_4$ cup) soft brown sugar
2 large eggs
250 g (9 oz/2 cups) plain (all-purpose) flour
1 teaspoon bicarbonate of soda (baking soda)
1^1/$_2$ teaspoons ground cinnamon
5–6 (about 900 g/2 lb) very ripe bananas, mashed
1 teaspoon natural vanilla extract
125 g (4^1/$_2$ oz/^{1}/$_2$ cup) sour cream
50 g (1^3/$_4$ oz/about ^{1}/$_2$ cup) walnuts, pecans or
   macadamia nuts, chopped, optional

BROWN SUGAR BUTTER
125 g (4^1/$_2$ oz) unsalted butter, softened
45 g (1^3/$_4$ oz/^{1}/$_4$ cup) dark brown sugar
1 teaspoon natural vanilla extract

makes 1 loaf (serves 6–8)

Preheat the oven to 160°C (315°F/Gas 2–3). Grease the base of a loaf (bar) tin approximately 22 cm (8^1/$_2$ inches) long, 9 cm (3^1/$_2$ inches) wide and 9 cm (3^1/$_2$ inches) deep. Line the base with baking paper.

Cream the butter with the caster sugar and brown sugar until light and fluffy. Beat in the eggs one at a time until well incorporated. Sift the flour, bicarbonate of soda and cinnamon with a pinch of salt, then beat it into the butter mixture to form a thick batter.

Combine the banana, vanilla and sour cream and fold into the butter mixture, with the nuts if using, until just combined. Pour into the prepared tin and smooth over the top. Bake for 1^1/$_4$ hours, or until a skewer inserted in the middle comes out clean. Allow to cool in the tin for 15 minutes, then invert onto a wire rack to cool to room temperature.

While the cake is cooling, make the brown sugar butter by beating the butter, sugar and vanilla until light and fluffy. (Do not refrigerate unless you are preparing the butter in advance, in which case remove it from the fridge before serving so it softens enough to spread easily.)

Thickly slice the banana bread using a bread knife or serrated knife. Toast and serve hot, spread with the brown sugar butter.

VARIATION: Top a slice of banana bread with thinly sliced banana, dollop with a little of the butter and place under a hot grill (broiler) until lightly golden.

A contemporary addition to café menus, this moist, dense, cake-like quickbread has been around for over 300 years, becoming popular with home cooks around the 1920s. Banana bread makes such an easy, light breakfast when teamed with a good coffee. Although pretty wonderful when freshly baked, it really shines when thick slabs of it are toasted and spread with butter. The contrast of the caramelized crispy edges with the soft, melty butter is divine. I wrap up and freeze individual slices so I can just pop some in the toaster whenever I crave it.

❋ scrambled eggs with asparagus & salmon roe,
    spicy baked beans &
banana bread with brown sugar butter

spicy baked beans

My dad used to sing a little ditty about baked beans but it isn't appropriate for print — well not in a cookbook anyway! The baked beans we eat today are believed to draw upon Native American as well as French or Italian origins. Baked beans were first produced commercially by the Americans in the late 1800s, with the British following close behind. Although the tinned form is very handy, it just doesn't compare with this flavoursome version, which is almost, but not quite, as quick as opening the tin.

1 tablespoon olive oil

1 small brown onion, chopped

1 slice of bacon, finely chopped, optional

1 garlic clove, crushed

60 g (2¼ oz/¼ cup) tomato paste (concentrated purée)

1 bay leaf

1 teaspoon sweet paprika (or smoked sweet paprika if not using bacon)

large pinch of cayenne pepper

2 teaspoons mustard powder

2 tablespoons worcestershire sauce

2 tablespoons golden syrup (if unavailable, substitute with 2 teaspoons each honey & dark corn syrup)

1½ teaspoons sea salt flakes

2 x 400 g (14 oz) tins cannellini beans, drained

serves 2 as a main, 4 as a side

Heat the olive oil in a saucepan over medium–high heat. Add the onion and the bacon, if using, and sauté for 5 minutes, or until lightly golden. Add the garlic, tomato paste, bay leaf, paprika, cayenne pepper, mustard powder, worcestershire sauce, golden syrup, sea salt flakes and 375 ml (13 fl oz/1½ cups) water. Stir well and bring to the boil, then reduce the heat and simmer for 10 minutes. Add the beans and cook, stirring occasionally, for a further 10–15 minutes, or until the mixture is thick and saucy and the beans are tender but not mushy.

Season to taste and serve on thick slabs of buttered toast or as a side dish for fried or poached eggs. These spicy baked beans also make a great jaffle filling (see page 13).

scrambled eggs
with asparagus & salmon roe

❊ *Although we tend to enjoy them first and foremost as a breakfast dish, many dressed-up versions of scrambled eggs are served all over the world and eaten at almost any time of the day. This recipe may seem quite a posh interpretation of the breakfast classic, but if you don't have a hankering for fresh asparagus and roe, you can simply serve the scrambled eggs on toast as they are divinely creamy and delicious on their own!*

8 large eggs
185 ml (6 fl oz/³/4 cup) pouring (whipping) cream
12 asparagus spears, ends trimmed
40 g (1¹/2 oz) butter
3 teaspoons snipped chives, plus extra, to garnish
1 teaspoon chopped dill, optional, plus extra,
    to garnish
2 tablespoons salmon roe

serves 4

Bring a saucepan of lightly salted water to the boil. Meanwhile, crack the eggs into a large jug or a bowl with a pouring lip, pour in the cream and whisk together just to combine. Add the asparagus to the boiling water and cook for 1 minute. Drain and cover with a clean tea towel (dish cloth) to keep warm.

Melt the butter in a large saucepan over medium heat. Stir the chives and dill, if using, into the eggs and season with a little salt and pepper. Pour the egg mixture into the pan and do not stir for 30 seconds. Reduce the heat slightly to medium–low, gently stir the eggs in a figure eight and leave again for another 30 seconds. Repeat this step until you have soft but glossy curds or clumps — this should take about 5 minutes. Remove from the heat. The eggs will continue to cook after they are taken off the heat, so don't worry if they still look a little undercooked — the eggs are not meant to be dry and too firm.

Serve three spears of the asparagus — over some buttered toast if you like — topped with a quarter of the scrambled egg. Garnish with a little salmon roe and extra chives or dill. Serve piping hot.

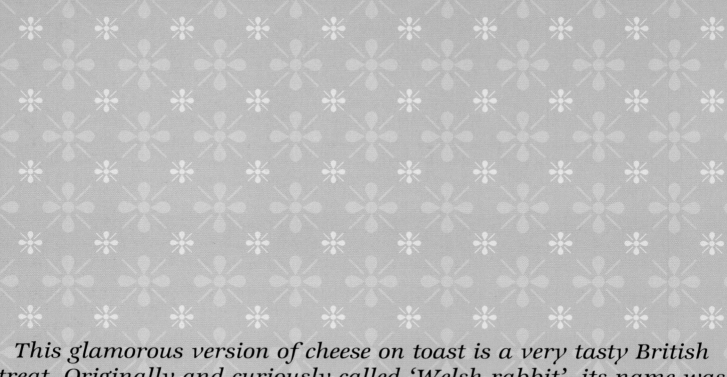

This glamorous version of cheese on toast is a very tasty British treat. Originally and curiously called 'Welsh rabbit', its name was changed to 'rarebit' sometime in the 1700s or 1800s, perhaps to avoid confusion over its true contents or in an effort to avoid perpetuating offence. Personally I am happy it's bunny free!

✳ welsh rarebit

RAREBIT SAUCE

175 g (6 oz/1²/₃ cups) grated sharp, crumbly
  cheddar cheese
1 tablespoon beer
1¹/₂ tablespoons milk or pouring (whipping) cream
10 g (¹/₄ oz) butter
1 teaspoon worcestershire sauce
¹/₂ teaspoon mustard powder
pinch of cayenne pepper
1 egg

30 g (1 oz) butter
1 garlic clove, finely chopped
300 g (10¹/₂ oz) baby English spinach leaves,
  rinsed and drained
1 teaspoon lemon juice
4 English muffins

serves 4

To make the rarebit sauce, put the cheese, beer, milk, butter, worcestershire sauce, mustard powder and cayenne pepper in a small saucepan and mix to combine well. Stir over low heat until the butter and cheese have just melted. Remove from the heat and beat in the egg. Season to taste and refrigerate just until the sauce is cool and of a nice spreadable consistency. If you're making the sauce in advance and it becomes too firm to spread, just give it a good whisk until it softens again.

Meanwhile, preheat the grill (broiler) to high. Melt the butter in a small frying pan over medium heat. Add the garlic and stir for 30 seconds, or until lightly golden. Add the spinach and a large pinch of salt and cook for 2 minutes, or until well wilted. Remove the spinach with a slotted spoon, discarding any juices. Drizzle the lemon juice over and toss to combine. Season with salt and freshly cracked black pepper.

While the spinach is wilting, split the muffins and place on a baking tray under the grill until lightly toasted.

Pile the hot spinach on top of the toasted muffins, then dollop on the rarebit sauce — spread it out slightly, but not right to the edges of the muffins as it will spread further while melting. Return to the grill and cook for 2–3 minutes, or until the sauce is lightly golden and bubbling. Serve immediately.

VARIATIONS: I have added some lightly wilted spinach here for contrast, but in a decadent mood I might top the rarebit with some smoked salmon or crabmeat, or bacon and a poached or fried egg. Note no bunny!

❋ *The soft, white, flour-dusted damper available in bakeries today bears little resemblance to the traditional version — a rudimentary paste of flour, water and salt that was moulded around a stick and cooked over a bush campfire until crusty. Not exactly gourmet but it filled a spot. No need to gather kindling here — just pull the damper out of a hot oven for a hearty, healthy breakfast.*

garlic mushrooms
& avocado on damper

DAMPER

500 g (1 lb 2 oz/4 cups) self-raising flour
1½ teaspoons salt
3 teaspoons sugar
2 tablespoons butter
250 ml (9 fl oz/1 cup) milk
250 ml (9 fl oz/1 cup) beer
1½ tablespoons plain (all-purpose) flour

2 tablespoons olive oil
50 g (1¾ oz) butter
4 garlic cloves, finely chopped
1 small red chilli, seeded & finely chopped, optional
500 g (1 lb 2 oz) flat mushrooms, stems trimmed & left whole, or thickly sliced if large
1 tablespoon finely chopped oregano
1 teaspoon sea salt flakes, plus extra, for sprinkling
1 handful of flat-leaf (Italian) parsley, roughly shredded
2 small, ripe avocados
1½ tablespoons lemon juice
extra virgin olive oil, for drizzling
flat-leaf (Italian) parsley, extra, to garnish

serves 4

Preheat the oven to 180°C (350°F/Gas 4). To make the damper, sift the self-raising flour, salt and sugar into a large bowl and stir to combine. Make a large well in the centre. Heat the butter and milk in a small saucepan over medium heat until the butter has melted, then pour into the well along with the beer.

Using a flat-bladed knife, drag the liquid towards the edges of the bowl, turning the bowl as you go, until the mixture forms a soft dough. Turn the dough out onto a lightly floured surface and knead for 5 minutes, or until smooth and silky to touch.

Grease a 20 cm (8 inch) round cake tin. Pat the damper into a round and shape it so it fits neatly inside the tin. Sift the plain flour over the damper, then cut a deep cross in the top. Bake for 35–40 minutes, or until lightly golden and hollow-sounding when tapped. Allow to cool slightly.

Meanwhile, heat the olive oil and 40 g (1½ oz) of the butter in a frying pan over medium–high heat. Add the garlic and chilli and stir for 30 seconds, or until the garlic is lightly golden. Add the mushrooms, oregano, sea salt flakes and 60 ml (2 fl oz/¼ cup) water. Reduce the heat and cook, stirring occasionally, for 8 minutes, or until the mushrooms are tender. Just before the mushrooms are cooked, cut the damper into thick slices using a serrated knife and lightly toast or grill (broil) them. Stir the remaining butter and the parsley through the mushrooms and season with freshly cracked black pepper.

Peel and remove the stones from the avocados. Cut each avocado into wedges and drizzle with a little of the lemon juice.

Pile the mushroom mixture over the toasted damper slices and top with avocado wedges. Drizzle with the remaining lemon juice and some extra virgin olive oil. Finish with a scattering of parsley, a good grind of fresh black pepper and a sprinkling of sea salt flakes.

bubble & squeak
patties with lamb cutlets

BUBBLE & SQUEAK PATTIES

30 g (1 oz) butter

1/2 small brown onion, finely chopped

1 large garlic clove, crushed

300 g (10 1/2 oz/1 1/4 cups) cooked potato,
   roughly mashed

1 cup very finely diced mixed cooked vegetables
   of your choice, such as pumpkin (winter squash),
   carrot, sweet potato, cabbage, brussels sprouts,
   broccoli & beans

1 small handful of flat-leaf (Italian) parsley, chopped

1 teaspoon finely chopped thyme

1 large egg

plain (all-purpose) flour, for coating

60 ml (2 fl oz/1/4 cup) olive oil

1/2 teaspoon finely chopped thyme

8 French-trimmed lamb cutlets (Frenched rib chops)

lemon wedges, to serve, optional

serves 4

To make the bubble and squeak patties, melt the butter in a saucepan over medium–high heat, add the onion and sauté for 5 minutes, or until lightly golden. Add the garlic and cook for 30 seconds. Remove from the pan and mix together with the mashed potato, finely chopped vegetables, parsley, thyme and egg. Season well, then refrigerate until firm. Divide into four even portions, then shape into patties about 8 cm (3 1/4 inches) wide and 2.5 cm (1 inch) thick. Lightly coat with flour.

Heat 2 1/2 tablespoons of the olive oil in a non-stick frying pan over medium heat and cook the patties for 4–5 minutes on each side, or until deeply golden and heated right through. Set aside and keep warm in a low oven.

Heat a large, heavy-based frying pan over medium–high heat. Combine the remaining olive oil with the thyme and rub it into the lamb cutlets, then season the cutlets on both sides with salt and freshly cracked black pepper. Fry the cutlets in the hot pan for 1 1/2 minutes on each side for a pink result, or until cooked to your liking. Transfer the cutlets to a plate and cover to keep warm while they rest for a few minutes.

Place one patty on each serving plate and lean two cutlets up against it. Serve with a lemon wedge if desired.

VARIATIONS: Top the patties with a poached or fried egg instead of the lamb. Also, you can add a handful of grated parmesan or sharp cheddar cheese to the patty mixture and top with some roasted tomatoes for a vegetarian option. Some finely chopped bacon or ham, or even some smoked salmon or drained tinned salmon, is also nice through the patty mixture — these patties are good enough to enjoy on their own!

'Bubble 'n' Squeak for breakfast, Bubble 'n' Squeak for tea, Bubble 'n' Squeak and caviar — just on its own for me!'
So went the jingle for a brand of frozen bubble and squeak, oh about 25 years ago now — and I still catch myself singing it every now and again. I really liked it as a kid if the home-made stuff wasn't on offer. Named for the sounds it makes while it is cooking, bubble and squeak is an English recipe, traditionally combining meat and vegetables left over from the previous night's dinner (usually a roast), fried until lightly golden. It should predominantly contain potato and cabbage, but you can throw in almost any lightly mashed or finely chopped vegetables or meat. While the lamb cutlets are a modern touch here and a bit extravagant — something you might enjoy in a nice café for brunch — it also makes for a good light dinner if you add a few more cutlets per person and serve with some steamed green beans.

Although it is traditionally served toasted as part of a proper English high tea, Australians have a fond attachment to this bubbly-looking, yeast-leavened version of the pancake. Making crumpets yourself is not only therapeutic, but a big reward in the eating. Truly, there is nothing quite like a home-made crumpet.

crumpets with ginger mascarpone, nectarines & golden syrup

CRUMPETS
2 teaspoons dried yeast
1 teaspoon caster (superfine) sugar
310 ml (10¾ fl oz/1¼ cups) warm milk
250 g (9 oz/2 cups) plain (all-purpose) flour
1 large egg, lightly beaten
¼ teaspoon bicarbonate of soda (baking soda)
vegetable oil, for cooking (choose one with a
   mild flavour)

3 tablespoons drained stem ginger in syrup,
   very finely chopped, plus 1 tablespoon of the syrup
250 g (9 oz/1 heaped cup) mascarpone cheese
4 ripe nectarines or small peaches, cut into
   thin wedges
golden syrup or honey, for drizzling

makes about 12 (serves 4–6)

To make the crumpets, sprinkle the yeast and sugar over 125 ml (4 fl oz/½ cup) of the warm milk and stir until the yeast has dissolved. Cover with a clean tea towel (dish towel) and leave to sit in a warm place for 15 minutes, or until frothy.

Sift the flour and 1 teaspoon salt into a bowl and make a well in the centre. Whisk the remaining milk with the egg and pour into the well. Add the yeast mixture, then whisk to form a smooth, soft batter. Cover with a tea towel and allow to rest in a warm place for 1 hour, or until the batter has doubled in volume and is covered with bubbles. Mix the bicarbonate of soda with 1 tablespoon water and beat it into the batter. Leave to rest for a further 10 minutes before cooking.

Meanwhile, mix the chopped ginger and ginger syrup through the mascarpone cheese and refrigerate until ready to serve.

Heat a large, heavy-based frying pan over medium heat. Brush with vegetable oil. Working in batches, carefully ladle ¼ cupfuls of the crumpet batter into the pan, leaving space in between for spreading. Cook for 5 minutes, or until the top is completely covered with popped bubbles and is dry to touch. If you like, flip the crumpets over and cook for a further 30 seconds, or until just very lightly golden. Remove from the pan and cover with a tea towel to keep warm while you cook the remainder. (You can also cook the mixture inside egg rings for a less rustic result, but you will need to use a little less mixture in each one.)

Serve two or three crumpets per plate, topped with a dollop of ginger marscapone, some nectarine slices and a drizzle of golden syrup. You can reheat any leftover crumpets by toasting or grilling (broiling) them.

VARIATION: For a savoury breakfast, smear the hot crumpets with butter and Vegemite or Marmite and top with a poached egg.

Who could resist such a marvellous breakfast combination? I love creamed spinach and sweet, oven-roasted tomatoes as individual breakfast items, but they also happen to make superb accompaniments to a fluffy, cheesy omelette. This isn't really a quick breakfast to prepare, but you can cook the tomatoes and the spinach ahead of time and simply reheat them. A decadent start to a lazy Sunday, or whenever you have time to relax and play! And nap.

✳ parmesan omelette
with creamed spinach &
roasted cherry tomatoes

ROASTED CHERRY TOMATOES

500 g (1 lb 2 oz) cherry tomatoes

2 teaspoons finely chopped thyme

4 garlic cloves, bruised & cut in half

1 teaspoon caster (superfine) sugar

1 tablespoon balsamic vinegar

2 tablespoons olive oil

1 teaspoon sea salt flakes

CREAMED SPINACH

300 g (10½ oz) English spinach leaves, rinsed

40 g (1½ oz) butter

½ small brown onion, finely chopped

1 garlic clove, crushed

2 teaspoons plain (all-purpose) flour

250 ml (9 fl oz/1 cup) pouring (whipping) cream

large pinch of freshly grated nutmeg

8 eggs

20 g (¾ oz) butter

35 g (1¼ oz/⅓ cup) finely grated parmesan cheese

serves 4

Preheat the oven to 180°C (350°F/Gas 4). To roast the cherry tomatoes, put them in a roasting tin with the thyme, garlic cloves, sugar, vinegar, olive oil and sea salt flakes and toss to combine well. Bake for 30 minutes, shaking the tin occasionally, until the tomatoes are slightly shrivelled. Discard the garlic cloves and cover to keep warm.

Meanwhile, make the creamed spinach. Put the spinach in a heatproof colander and pour boiling water over the top to wilt the leaves, then allow to cool. Melt the butter in a frying pan over medium–high heat, add the onion and sauté for 5 minutes, or until lightly golden. Add the garlic and cook for a further 30 seconds. Stir in the flour and cook for 1 minute, then stir in the cream. Bring to the boil and stir continuously for 1–2 minutes, or until thickened. Squeeze any excess water from the spinach, then chop the spinach and add it to the cream mixture with the nutmeg. Season to taste, then turn off the heat.

To make the omelettes, whisk the eggs and 80 ml (2½ fl oz/⅓ cup) water together in a jug. Melt a quarter of the butter in a small non-stick frying pan over medium heat. Pour in a quarter of the beaten eggs. After a minute, or when the egg starts to just cook on the bottom, use a wooden spoon to drag the egg mixture from the outside edges in towards the centre. Tilt the pan slightly, allowing the raw mixture to run back into the gaps. Repeat this process until the egg stops flowing freely. Cook for a further minute, then sprinkle a tablespoon of the parmesan over the top and gently fold one half of the omelette over the other, forming a half-moon. Cook for a further 30 seconds, then slide the omelette out onto a baking tray. Cover and keep warm in a very low oven while you make the remaining three omelettes.

Meanwhile, gently reheat the creamed spinach. Serve each omelette topped with the creamed spinach and the roasted tomatoes. Serve immediately.

❊ *Middle Eastern couscous with hot milk, dried fruit and nuts has become rather trendy for breakfast in recent years, but here it takes on a Southeast Asian twist, cooked with coconut milk and topped with an exquisite fruit salad with refreshing ginger and mint. A multicultural breakfast indeed!*

coconut couscous
with fruit in ginger mint syrup

GINGER MINT SYRUP

55 g (2 oz/1/3 cup) caster (superfine) sugar
50 g (1³/4 oz) fresh ginger, peeled & sliced thinly
1/2 vanilla bean, split lengthways
1 large mint sprig

1/2 small ripe rockmelon, or other orange-fleshed
    melon, cut into 2 cm (³/4 inch) cubes
1/2 small honeydew melon, cut into
    2 cm (³/4 inch) cubes
1/2 small sweet, ripe pineapple, cut into
    2 cm (³/4 inch) cubes
16 ripe lychees, peeled
1 starfruit, thinly sliced
1 handful of tiny mint leaves, or 1 small handful
    of finely shredded mint
toasted shredded coconut, to garnish, optional
coconut cream, to serve, optional

COCONUT COUSCOUS

800 ml (28 fl oz) coconut milk
2 tablespoons caster (superfine) sugar
1 teaspoon salt
370 g (13 oz/2 cups) couscous

serves 6

To make the ginger mint syrup, put the sugar and 500 ml (17 fl oz/ 2 cups) water in a small saucepan and stir over high heat until the sugar has dissolved. Add the ginger, vanilla bean and mint sprig and bring to the boil, then reduce the heat and simmer for 15–20 minutes, or until slightly syrupy. Cool to room temperature.

Combine the melons, pineapple, lychees and starfruit and strain the syrup over the top. Stir in half the mint, then refrigerate for at least 2 hours, stirring occasionally.

When ready to serve, make the coconut couscous. Put the coconut milk, sugar and salt in a saucepan and bring to the boil. Turn off the heat, immediately stir in the couscous and cover with a lid. Allow to sit for 3 minutes for the coconut milk to be absorbed, then fluff up the grains with a fork.

Serve the couscous immediately in a wide, shallow bowl topped with the fruit and drizzled with the syrup. Garnish with the remaining mint and the toasted coconut, if using. Serve with a small jug of coconut cream on the side for drizzling over if desired.

NOTE: If the couscous is left sitting you will need to add extra coconut milk when you reheat it so it is not too dry.

VARIATION: The couscous is also great simply served with fresh mango chunks or banana slices, perhaps with a little coconut cream drizzled over the top.

*on the BARBECUE

AH, THE BACKYARD BARBECUE — ICONIC OUTDOOR COOKWARE AT ITS BEST. WHAT BETTER WAY TO CONCRETE FRIENDSHIP THAN BY SIZZLING A SAUSAGE ON THE BARBECUE WHILE ENJOYING A BEER OR THREE AND SOAKING UP THE SUNSHINE? I SOMETIMES PONDER WHY IT IS PREDOMINANTLY THE MALE OF THE SPECIES THAT CONGREGATES AROUND THE BARBECUE — PERHAPS A REFERENCE CHECK ON CAVEMEN AND FIRES MIGHT FILL IN THE GAPS! — BUT IT IS NEVERTHELESS APPARENT THAT THE BARBECUE IS OFTEN THE MAN'S DOMAIN, COMPLETE WITH BRAGGING RIGHTS, AND AS LONG AS ALL THE PREPARATION IS DONE FOR THEM BEFOREHAND AND THE CLEAN-UP AFTERWARDS IT WILL REMAIN AS SUCH.

THE BARBECUE IS ACTUALLY A FANTASTIC COOKING DEVICE AND I ENCOURAGE EVERYONE TO USE IT FREQUENTLY — AND FOR MUCH MORE THAN STEAKS AND SAUSAGES AND THE OCCASIONAL PRAWN. BE ADVENTUROUS AND COMPLEMENT PERFECTLY COOKED MEATS WITH A GENEROUS SELECTION OF WONDERFUL SALADS AND SIDES FOR THE VERY BEST WAY TO SPEND TIME WITH GOOD FRIENDS AND FAMILY IN THE OUTDOORS, DAY OR EVENING — JUST DON'T FORGET THE INSECT REPELLENT...

* french onion dip * corn relish dip * barbecued chicken with lemon & basil aioli * garlic king prawns * tuna steaks with bush tomato jam * salmon fillets with caper, cheddar & pickled onion butter * lamb burger with beetroot relish & tahini cream * whole baby snapper with herb & macadamia salsa * steak sandwich with boozy onions * barbecued lobster with thai dressing & cucumber salad * steak with vegemite butter * peppered lamb cutlets with sweet shiraz glaze * couscous salad * eggplant with goat's feta & oregano dressing * spinach, pancetta & pear salad with balsamic dressing * spiced beetroot salad * asian coleslaw * potato salad * green bean salad with artichokes * pasta salad * roast pumpkin & rocket salad with creamy mustard dressing * summer punch

french onion dip

This was 'the' dip to serve in the 70s and early 80s, a savoury concoction made by stirring a packet of French onion soup mix into a carton of sour cream. I adored that dip as a kid, but as my love of cooking and food evolved I learned to appreciate the freshness and flavour of foods made from scratch — and so this new and improved version was born. Sure it takes a little longer to make, but if you are a 'French onion' fan you will love this dip — and won't you just feel better knowing it didn't fall out of a packet?

1 tablespoon olive oil
2 brown onions, cut into quarters & finely sliced
large pinch of sugar
300 g (10½ oz/1¼ cups) sour cream
60 g (2¼ oz/¼ cup) whole-egg mayonnaise
1 tablespoon dijon mustard
1 tablespoon worcestershire sauce
1 garlic clove, crushed
pinch of cayenne pepper
½ teaspoon celery salt
¼ teaspoon dried sage
1 small handful of flat-leaf (Italian) parsley, finely chopped

makes 2 cups (500 g/1 lb 2 oz)

Heat the olive oil in a large frying pan over medium heat and add the onion, sugar and a large pinch of salt. Cook, stirring regularly, for 30 minutes, or until the onion is dark golden. Take off the heat and allow to cool completely.

Mix the sour cream, mayonnaise, mustard, worcestershire sauce, garlic, cayenne pepper, celery salt, sage and parsley together until thoroughly combined. Add the cooled onion and mix well. Season to taste. Chill until ready to serve.

Serve with savoury biscuits (crackers) or vegetable crudités — my favourites for this dip are crisp cucumber, celery and baby carrots.

corn relish dip

Unless lucky enough to snap up a jar of corn relish made by someone's grandmother from a local fete, most of us are reduced to buying corn relish straight off the supermarket shelf. Fear not, this relish is easy to make using fresh corn, vinegar and spices. It is equally fabulous as a slightly sweet, tangy dip when mixed with sour cream — as in the recipe below — or on its own as a condiment with cold meats or in sandwiches. It's one of those old-fashioned dips that you'll want to make again and again.

2 tablespoons olive oil

1 small red onion, finely chopped

400 g (14 oz/2 cups) fresh corn kernels
(about 2 cobs of corn)

1 tablespoon mustard powder

1½ teaspoons brown mustard seeds

¼ teaspoon ground cumin

½ red capsicum (pepper), finely chopped

½ celery stalk

2 garlic cloves, crushed

125 ml (4 fl oz/½ cup) cider vinegar

½ teaspoon Tabasco sauce

2½ tablespoons soft brown sugar

160 g (5¾ oz/⅔ cup) sour cream

makes 2 cups (650 g/1 lb 7 oz)

Heat the olive oil in a heavy-based saucepan over high heat. Add the onion and corn. Cook, stirring frequently to prevent catching and burning, for 10 minutes, or until the onion is soft and there is a golden film on the bottom of the pan. Add the mustard powder, mustard seeds and cumin and stir until fragrant. Add the capsicum, celery, garlic, vinegar, Tabasco, sugar, 125 ml (4 fl oz/½ cup) water and 1 teaspoon salt and bring to the boil, scraping up any caramelized bits. Reduce the heat and simmer for 45 minutes, or until the corn is tender and almost all the liquid has evaporated. Take off the heat and allow to cool completely.

Tip the relish into a food processor and blend until roughly chopped. Put the sour cream in a serving bowl, mix the relish through and season to taste. Serve with strips of toasted pide (Turkish/flat) bread or melba toasts, savoury biscuits (crackers) or vegetable crudités.

✳ *The glorious Italians brought us amazing pasta dishes, wonderful salami, fresh fennel sausages, great bread, cheese, pizza and coffee — but we are also indebted to them for introducing us to the essential flavours of garlic and basil, now staples in our diet. Often found growing in backyard herb gardens, fresh, sweet basil thrives in the warmer months, and is fabulous in everything from pesto to salads. I adore it in the dish below, perfuming the lush, lemony chicken with its fresh, faintly aniseedy leaves.*

barbecued chicken
with lemon & basil aioli

4 x 200 g (7 oz) boneless, skinless chicken breasts
2 tablespoons lemon juice
60 ml (2 fl oz/1/4 cup) olive oil
4 garlic cloves, bruised
1 small handful of basil leaves, shredded
3 red capsicums (peppers)

LEMON & BASIL AIOLI
125 g (4 1/2 oz/1/2 cup) whole-egg mayonnaise
1 1/2 tablespoons lemon juice
3 garlic cloves, crushed
1 small handful of basil, finely shredded

serves 4

Slice the chicken breasts through the middle to form two smaller breasts. Place each piece of chicken between two slices of plastic wrap and beat with a meat mallet or rolling pin until about 5 mm (1/4 inch) thick. Combine the lemon juice, olive oil, garlic cloves and basil in a large, non-metallic baking dish. Add the chicken pieces and mix to coat well. Cover and refrigerate overnight.

Mix all the lemon and basil aioli ingredients together in a small bowl and refrigerate until ready to use.

Preheat a barbecue grill plate to high. Cut each capsicum into quarters and trim the curled ends so that they become flattish pieces. Remove the seeds and membranes. Grill the capsicum, skin side down, for 10 minutes, or until the skin side is blackened and blistered and the flesh is tender. Remove to a plate, cover tightly with foil and leave to rest while the chicken is cooking.

Remove the chicken from the marinade, discarding the marinade. Season the chicken with a little salt and freshly cracked black pepper and grill for 1 1/2 minutes on each side, or until just cooked through. Remove from the heat, cover loosely with foil and allow to rest for 5 minutes.

While the chicken is resting, peel the skin from the capsicum quarters and discard. Serve two chicken pieces and three capsicum quarters per person and dollop with the lemon and basil aioli. Terrific with a green salad.

Every barbecue hotplate has to be christened at some stage with a clutch of fat, juicy prawns! Cooking them in their shells is great for time-poor chefs, but unfortunately rather messy for diners to peel. Here the work is done for your guests — and as a special treat, the prawns are tossed with a rich, garlicky butter. If, like me, you are a fan of restaurant-style garlic prawns, but don't, like most of us, own those little lidded cast-iron pots, this recipe was designed with you in mind.

✳ garlic king prawns

GARLIC BUTTER

60 g (2 1/4 oz) butter, softened
1 small red chilli, seeded & finely chopped
3 garlic cloves, crushed
2 anchovies, very finely chopped
1 tablespoon brandy
1 1/2 teaspoons sea salt flakes

1.5 kg (3 lb 5 oz) king (jumbo) prawns (shrimp),
   peeled & deveined, with tails intact
4 garlic cloves, bruised well
1 1/2 teaspoons finely grated lemon zest
60 ml (2 fl oz/1/4 cup) olive oil
1 large handful of flat-leaf (Italian) parsley, chopped
lemon cheeks, to serve

serves 6

Thoroughly combine all the garlic butter ingredients, then cover and refrigerate overnight for the flavours to develop well.

Put the prawns in a bowl with the garlic, lemon zest and olive oil and toss to coat well. Cover and refrigerate for a few hours to allow the flavours to develop.

When you're ready to cook, preheat a barbecue flatplate to medium–high. Pick the garlic cloves out of the prawns and spread the prawns on the flatplate in a single layer. Grill the prawns, turning occasionally, for 3–4 minutes, or until just cooked through. Transfer the prawns to a bowl. Dice the garlic butter and toss through the prawns until the butter is almost melted. Add the parsley, toss well and season to taste.

Serve with lemon cheeks for squeezing over, either as a starter or as part of a buffet.

NOTE: To make a more substantial meal, pile the prawns on top of some fresh damper (see page 32) and serve with a green salad.

✳ garlic king prawns,
   salmon fillets with caper, cheddar & pickled onion butter
& tuna steaks with bush tomato jam

tuna steaks
with bush tomato jam

BUSH TOMATO JAM

80 ml (2½ fl oz/⅓ cup) olive oil

1 large brown onion, chopped

3 teaspoons yellow or brown mustard seeds

1 teaspoon ground mountain pepperleaf or
   ground oregano

1 garlic clove, crushed

800 g (1 lb 12 oz) very ripe tomatoes, peeled,
   seeded & chopped (see Note)

80 ml (2½ fl oz/⅓ cup) red wine vinegar

2½ teaspoons ground akudjura (bush tomato powder),
   or 1 tablespoon finely chopped sun-dried tomato

2½ tablespoons soft brown sugar

4 x 200 g (7 oz) tuna steaks

olive oil, for brushing

lime cheeks, to serve, optional

baby rocket (arugula) leaves, to serve

serves 4

To make the bush tomato jam, heat the olive oil in a saucepan over medium heat. Add the onion and sauté for 15 minutes, or until golden. Stir in the mustard seeds and cook for 1 minute. Add the pepperleaf and garlic and cook for a further 30 seconds, or until fragrant. Add the chopped tomatoes, vinegar, akudjura and ¼ teaspoon salt and bring to the boil. Reduce the heat and simmer for 1 hour, or until thick and pulpy. Add the sugar and turn the heat down to very, very low, so the jam is barely simmering — use a heat diffuser if necessary. Cook, stirring regularly to ensure the jam doesn't stick and burn, for a further 3 hours, or until the mixture is thick, dark and jammy and oil starts to pool on the top.

Heat a barbecue grill plate to high. Brush the tuna steaks with a little olive oil and season with salt and freshly cracked black pepper. Grill the tuna for 1½ minutes on each side for a rare result, or until cooked to your liking. Serve the tuna topped with a dollop of the bush tomato jam, some lime cheeks and a tumble of rocket leaves on the side — you can dress the rocket with a little lemon juice and olive oil if you like. Any leftover jam can be spread on a sandwich as a relish, or served with barbecued or pan-fried meats.

NOTE: To peel tomatoes, score a cross in the base of each tomato and put them in a heatproof bowl. Cover with boiling water, leave for 30 seconds, then plunge the tomatoes in cold water and peel the skin away from the cross.

The bush tomato or akudjura is not actually a tomato, but a native Australian berry with a sweet–sour flavour. Available dried and ground, it is great for boosting tomato-based dishes or relishes — such as this lusciously rich tomato jam — and makes a tangy seasoning for grilled foods. If unavailable, a small quantity of sun-dried tomato can be used instead. Mountain pepperleaf, also indigenous to Australia, further scents the jam, but if you can't find it, dried oregano has a similar flavour and aroma. Bush tomato and mountain pepperleaf are available through some speciality spice shops, gourmet emporiums and 'bush tucker' websites.

It's considered culinary suicide these days to serve cubes of cheddar cheese and cocktail-sized pickled onions speared onto toothpicks as an appetizer — but let's face it, the flavours were pretty damn good together. So, in honour of yet another 70s party-starter, I developed this tasty, slightly sharp butter to serve alongside tender fillets of luscious salmon, one of the few fish that can take the bold flavours. If salmon doesn't float your boat, try the butter with swordfish or chicken.

❉ salmon fillets
with caper, cheddar & pickled onion butter

60 g (2¼ oz) butter, softened
2 teaspoons capers in vinegar, rinsed & chopped
30 g (1 oz/about 2) pickled onions, finely chopped
50 g (1¾ oz/½ cup) grated mature cheddar cheese
1 tablespoon finely shredded parsley
4 x 180–200 g (6–7 oz) salmon fillets
olive oil, for brushing

serves 4

Mash together the butter, capers, pickled onion, cheese and parsley. Set aside. (If the weather is particularly warm, refrigerate the butter, but take it out of the fridge 20 minutes before serving so it can soften up.)

Heat a barbecue grill plate to medium–high. Brush the salmon all over with olive oil. Grill for 3 minutes on each side, or until cooked to your liking. Ideally the salmon should still be a little rare inside so it doesn't dry out too much.

Put a dollop or slice of the butter on each salmon fillet, letting it melt over the top. Serve with green beans and boiled baby potatoes.

✳ *I just don't 'do' beetroot on my hamburger — except as a zippy beetroot relish on a juicy lamb burger. For a simpler version, use beef instead of lamb, leave out the spices and top with your regular salad ingredients (including beetroot slices if you must). Don't tell anyone but I actually like pineapple on mine!*

lamb burger with
beetroot relish & tahini cream

LAMB BURGERS

500 g (1 lb 2 oz) minced (ground) lamb

120 g (4¼ oz/1½ cups) fresh breadcrumbs

1 small brown onion, grated, with the excess moisture squeezed out

3 garlic cloves, crushed

2 teaspoons ground cumin

1 teaspoon sweet paprika

½ teaspoon cayenne pepper

1½ teaspoons sea salt flakes

2 tablespoons tomato paste (concentrated purée)

1 teaspoon finely grated lemon zest

1 egg

BEETROOT RELISH

60 ml (2 fl oz/¼ cup) red wine vinegar

1 tablespoon honey

½ teaspoon ground cinnamon

¼ teaspoon ground allspice

1 teaspoon black mustard seeds

1 beetroot (beet), about 8 cm (3¼ inches) in diameter, peeled & grated

TAHINI CREAM

1 tablespoon tahini

60 g (2¼ oz/¼ cup) thick Greek-style yoghurt

2 garlic cloves, crushed

1 teaspoon lemon juice

2 small Lebanese (short) cucumbers

1 handful of mint, chopped

olive oil, for brushing

1 long pide (Turkish/flat) bread, or 6 individual pitta breads

To make the lamb burgers, thoroughly combine all the burger ingredients and shape into six even balls. Flatten them into 1.5 cm (5/8 inch) thick ovals and place on a tray lined with plastic wrap. Cover and refrigerate for at least 6 hours or overnight for the flavours to develop.

Put all the beetroot relish ingredients in a small saucepan with 185 ml (6 fl oz/3/4 cup) water and a teaspoon of salt. Stir well over high heat until the honey has dissolved. Bring to the boil, then reduce to a very slow simmer and cook, stirring occasionally, for 1¼ hours, or until most of the liquid has evaporated and the beetroot is tender. Take off the heat and allow to cool.

Meanwhile, combine all the tahini cream ingredients until smooth and refrigerate until ready to use. Season to taste. Finely slice the cucumbers and toss with the mint. Refrigerate until ready to use.

Preheat a barbecue flatplate to medium–high. Smear the burgers with a little olive oil and grill for 3–4 minutes on each side, or until cooked through. Cover and keep warm. If using a pide, cut it into six equal pieces, then split each through the middle. (If you like, brush the cut sides of the pide with olive oil and lightly toast them, cut side down, on the ridged grill plate.) If using round pitta breads, cut one edge to make a pocket so you can fill them.

Smear the cut sides of the pide slices with the tahini cream, then top each with some cucumber salad, a burger and a little beetroot relish. Place the bread tops on the burgers and serve. If using pitta breads, just fill them in any order you like.

VARIATION: For a vegetarian burger, try barbecued eggplant (aubergine) slices in place of the lamb burger.

serves 6

I am so fortunate to live in a country with such fresh, fine seafood on its shores. Snapper is a deliciously buttery, mildly flavoured fish that is equally at home with a fresh, herby dressing or a simple squeeze of lemon juice. Whole baby snapper are great for individual portions, but one large snapper would also work well — just wrap it in a double thickness of foil and adjust the cooking time according to its weight (check with your seafood monger for advice on cooking times). You can also bake the fish if your barbecue is on the blink or you get rained out.

whole baby snapper with herb & macadamia salsa

HERB & MACADAMIA SALSA

40 g (1½ oz/¼ cup) lightly toasted macadamia nuts, finely chopped
3 anchovies, very finely chopped
2 garlic cloves, crushed
1 large handful of flat-leaf (Italian) parsley, finely chopped
1 large handful of basil, finely chopped
1 handful of mint, finely chopped
½ teaspoon finely grated lemon zest
1 tablespoon lemon juice
125 ml (4 fl oz/½ cup) extra virgin olive oil
1 teaspoon sea salt flakes

4 whole baby snapper, about 500 g (1 lb 2 oz) each, scaled & cleaned
olive oil, for brushing
sea salt flakes, for sprinkling
lemon wedges, to serve

serves 4

Combine all the herb and macadamia salsa ingredients in a bowl. Season with freshly cracked black pepper and set aside for the flavours to develop.

Preheat a barbecue flatplate to medium–high. Make several deep slashes through the fleshiest part on both sides of each fish. Brush both sides with olive oil and sprinkle lightly with sea salt flakes.

Grill the snapper for 4–5 minutes on each side, or until the flesh is opaque. Be very careful when you turn the fish as it will tend to stick to the barbecue plate — this makes things a little messy, so if you prefer, wrap the fish in foil first, although the flavour will be more delicate if cooked this way.

Serve the fish with the salsa on the side for spooning over, and lemon wedges for squeezing over. Some crusty bread and a simple green salad make this a light and easy meal.

✳ *Steak sandwiches can be really sublime or a great disappointment. The key is using good-quality, fresh ingredients — without them you can end up with an unappealing, dry-as-a-bone jaw-breaker. The onions here are caramelized with a little beer — which everyone knows is the quintessential barbecue seasoning! — and the savoury mayonnaise makes a nice change from the usual tomato or barbecue sauce (but feel free to use them if you prefer). Don't forget to serve with an ice-cold beer.*

steak sandwich
with boozy onions

BOOZY ONIONS

1 tablespoon olive oil

2 brown onions, sliced

3 teaspoons soft brown sugar

80 ml (2$^{1}/_{2}$ fl oz/$^{1}/_{3}$ cup) beer of your choice — preferably the one you'll be drinking while turning the steaks!

1 teaspoon finely chopped thyme

WORCESTERSHIRE & MUSTARD MAYO

125 g (4$^{1}/_{2}$ oz/$^{1}/_{2}$ cup) good-quality whole-egg mayonnaise

1 tablespoon worcestershire sauce

1 garlic clove, crushed

2 teaspoons dijon mustard

8 thin slices of sourdough bread

olive oil, for brushing

400 g (14 oz) piece of fillet steak, cut into 5 mm ($^{1}/_{4}$ inch) slices (see Note)

2 small ripe tomatoes, thinly sliced

mixed baby salad leaves, to serve

serves 4

To make the boozy onions, heat the olive oil in a saucepan over medium heat. Add the onion and a large pinch of salt and cook for 30 minutes, or until lightly golden, stirring regularly. Add the sugar, beer and thyme and bring to the boil. Reduce to a slow simmer and cook, stirring regularly so the onion doesn't stick and burn, for a further 1 hour, or until the onion is well caramelized and darker in colour. Set aside.

In a small bowl, combine all the worcestershire and mustard mayo ingredients. Refrigerate until ready to use.

Preheat a barbecue grill plate to high. Lightly brush one side of the bread slices with olive oil, then briefly cook that side on the barbecue until light grill marks appear. Set aside, covered with foil to keep warm.

Season the steak slices with salt and pepper and cook for 45 seconds on each side, or until well seared. Be careful not to overcook them — they are best a little pink inside to stay tender.

Generously smear the non-grilled sides of the bread with the worcestershire and mustard mayo, then layer with some steak, boozy onions, tomato slices and salad leaves. Top with the other slices of bread to make four steak sandwiches.

NOTE: The beef will be easier to slice thinly if you partially freeze it first for about an hour.

They may be rather larger than prawns, but these fellas are great thrown on the barbecue too. The flavours in the dressing are influenced by Thai cuisine, where hot, sweet, sour and salty are always in perfect balance. The dressing has just a little bite, so if you like things really spicy add another chilli. The cooling cucumber salad is the perfect accompaniment — a wonderful summer's treat to share with those you wish to spoil.

barbecued lobster
with thai dressing &
cucumber salad

THAI DRESSING
1/2 teaspoon sesame oil
60 ml (2 fl oz/1/4 cup) vegetable oil
1 tablespoon fish sauce
60 ml (2 fl oz/1/4 cup) lime juice
1 small red chilli, seeded & very finely chopped
2 garlic cloves, crushed
3 makrut (kaffir lime) leaves, shredded
1 lemon grass stem, white part only, finely chopped
1/2 teaspoon finely grated fresh ginger
2 1/2 teaspoons shaved palm sugar (jaggery) or soft
  brown sugar
1 small handful of coriander (cilantro) leaves,
  finely chopped

CUCUMBER SALAD
3 Lebanese (short) cucumbers
3 red Asian shallots, very finely sliced
1 large handful of whole coriander (cilantro) leaves
1 handful of mint leaves, torn into small pieces

4 large lobster or crayfish tails in the shell
  (about 400 g/14 oz each)
lime wedges, to serve

**serves 4 as a main,
8 as a starter**

To make the Thai dressing, combine all the ingredients except 1 teaspoon of the palm sugar and all the coriander in a small bowl. Mix well to dissolve the sugar, then set aside for 2–3 hours for the flavours to develop. Strain through a sieve, pressing on the solids to extract as much liquid as possible. Pour half the dressing into a small bowl and reserve for basting the seafood. Add the remaining palm sugar and all the coriander to the remaining dressing and mix until the sugar has dissolved. Season to taste — this will be for dressing the lobster after cooking.

To make the cucumber salad, use a mandolin, vegetable peeler or very sharp knife to cut the cucumbers into long, thin ribbons. Gently toss in a bowl with the shallot and herbs and refrigerate until ready to serve.

Heat the barbecue grill plate to medium. Using a sharp, heavy knife, cut through the lobster or crayfish tails lengthways and remove the digestive tract. Brush the exposed meat liberally with the basting mixture and place on the grill plate, flesh side down. Grill for 4 minutes, then turn over and brush the flesh again with the remaining baste. Continue to cook, shell side down, for a further 7–8 minutes, or until the shells turn bright red.

Serve the tails with the cucumber salad and drizzle the coriander dressing over both. Serve lime wedges on the side for squeezing over. A small bowl of jasmine rice makes the meal complete.

steak
with vegemite butter

80 g (2³/₄ oz) softened butter
3 teaspoons Vegemite, or other yeast extract
   such as Marmite or Promite
1 garlic clove, crushed
1 teaspoon finely chopped thyme
4 x 200 g (7 oz) fillet steaks
olive oil, for brushing

serves 4

Combine the butter with the Vegemite, garlic and thyme and season with freshly cracked black pepper. Pat into a log and wrap in plastic wrap. Twist the ends of the plastic wrap in opposite directions to help form a smooth sausage, or pat into a rectangular shape. Refrigerate until ready to use, but bring to room temperature 5–10 minutes before serving to soften slightly.

Heat a barbecue grill plate to high. Brush the steaks with a little olive oil, then season with salt and freshly cracked black pepper. Grill the steaks for 3–4 minutes on each side, or until cooked to your liking. Remove from the heat, cover loosely with foil and allow to rest for 5 minutes. Slice the butter and place several discs on top of each steak.

Serve with potatoes and a green salad, or a mixture of lightly cooked green vegetables such as snow peas (mangetout), asparagus, baby green beans and perhaps some baby carrots.

It may seem an odd combination, but a perfectly chargrilled piece of beef fillet is wonderful with a dollop of rich, earthy Vegemite butter melting into it. I find that it's a fun thing to serve international guests who often believe Vegemite to be an 'acquired' taste. As with its cousins Marmite and Promite, this thick, dark, salty paste is made from a concentrated yeast extract and is packed full of vitamin B.

❋ I do indeed live in the lucky country when it comes to flavoursome, tender lamb. A short cooking time is all that is needed for these luscious cutlets. Good and peppery, they marry well with the fruity shiraz glaze, which is itself infused with a distinct peppery flavour owing to a generous splash of its namesake wine. No prize for guessing which wine you might serve with this!

peppered lamb cutlets
with sweet shiraz glaze

SWEET SHIRAZ GLAZE
500 ml (17 fl oz/2 cups) shiraz, or other red wine
4 French shallots, chopped
1 small rosemary sprig
100 g (3½ oz/⅓ cup) redcurrant jelly

12 lamb cutlets (rib chops)
2 tablespoons olive oil
3 teaspoons freshly cracked black pepper
2 teaspoons sea salt flakes

serves 4

To make the sweet shiraz glaze, put the wine, shallot and rosemary in a small saucepan and bring to the boil over high heat. Reduce the heat and simmer for 18–20 minutes, or until reduced by half. Add the redcurrant jelly and cook for a further 10 minutes, or until slightly glazy. Strain the mixture into a small jug, pressing on the solids to extract as much liquid as possible.

Preheat a barbecue flatplate to high. Brush the cutlets with a little olive oil, then rub them all over with the combined pepper and sea salt flakes. Grill the lamb for 2 minutes on each side for a pink result, or until cooked to your liking. Remove from the heat, cover loosely with foil and allow to rest for 5 minutes.

Serve the cutlets with the glaze on the side for pouring over. Great with steamed asparagus or green beans, or a simple green salad.

Couscous salads make a pretty impressive alternative to old-fashioned rice salads which, let's face it, can be pretty heavy. Only a relatively recent addition to Western supermarkets and pantries, granular couscous is light, nutty and, best of all, requires almost no cooking — perfect on a hot, hot day. It makes sense to showcase its Middle Eastern origins with complementary ingredients such as preserved lemon, which lends this salad an earthy, aromatic, punchy flavour, balanced with sweet raisins, lots of fresh herbs and crunchy pistachios.

COUSCOUS salad

125 ml (4 fl oz/½ cup) extra virgin olive oil
280 g (10 oz/1½ cups) couscous
50 g (1¾ oz/⅓ cup) pistachio nuts, chopped
2 preserved lemon quarters, flesh removed,
  & the rind rinsed & finely chopped
400 g (14 oz) tin chickpeas, drained
30 g (1 oz/¼ cup) raisins, chopped
2 spring onions (scallions), sliced
2 celery stalks, finely diced
1 large handful of flat-leaf (Italian) parsley,
  shredded
2 large handfuls of mint, finely shredded
1 large handful of coriander (cilantro) leaves,
  finely shredded
80 ml (2½ fl oz/⅓ cup) lemon juice
1 garlic clove, crushed

serves 6

Put 375 ml (13 fl oz/1½ cups) water in a large saucepan with 2 teaspoons salt and 2 tablespoons of the extra virgin olive oil. Bring just to the boil and remove from the heat. Stir in the couscous. Cover with a lid and set aside for a few minutes, then fluff up the couscous grains with a fork.

Stir in the pistachios, preserved lemon, chickpeas, raisins, spring onion, celery and herbs.

Combine the remaining extra virgin olive oil with the lemon juice and garlic, then pour over the couscous. Toss well, season to taste with salt and plenty of freshly ground black pepper and serve.

※on the barbecue [page 069]

*eggplant with goat's feta & oregano dressing

2 large, even-shaped eggplants (aubergines)

olive oil, for brushing

1/2 teaspoon finely grated lemon zest

2 tablespoons lemon juice

2 tablespoons extra virgin olive oil

1 garlic clove, crushed

1 small red chilli, seeded & finely sliced

1/2 teaspoon soft brown sugar

1 tablespoon finely chopped oregano, plus extra oregano leaves, to garnish

100 g (31/2 oz) goat's cheese feta marinated in olive oil (reserve some of the oil)

serves 6–8

Cut the eggplants in half lengthways, then slice into half-moons about 2 cm (3/4 inch) thick. Heat a barbecue grill plate to medium–high. Brush the eggplant slices with olive oil and sprinkle with a little salt. Grill for 10 minutes, turning regularly, until golden brown and tender. Remove from the heat.

Meanwhile, combine the lemon zest, lemon juice, extra virgin olive oil, garlic, chilli, sugar and chopped oregano in a small bowl and whisk to combine. Season to taste with salt and plenty of freshly cracked black pepper.

Pour the dressing over the eggplant while it is still warm and toss lightly to combine. Transfer to a serving platter and crumble the feta over the top. Drizzle with a little of the reserved marinating oil, sprinkle with some whole oregano leaves and serve.

With Australia home to one of the largest Greek communities outside Greece, it should come as no surprise that there has been some influence on Australian everyday cooking. Here is a great side dish to serve with another Grecian favourite, grilled lamb, but it also stands alone as a brilliant vegetarian main, perhaps served with a Mediterranean-inspired rice salad seasoned with spring onion, raisins, pine nuts, parsley and some finely shredded vine leaves in brine. Opa!

❉ spinach, pancetta & pear salad with balsamic dressing,
spiced beetroot salad &
asian coleslaw

spinach, pancetta & pear salad with balsamic dressing

I first cooked a warm version of this salad in the late 80s at a dinner party I was catering for. The client had requested it as a starter. I hadn't made it before but was very impressed with the outcome — it was so simple and delicious and the guests absolutely loved it. I'll now own up to snacking on more than a few pieces of crispy pancetta before the salad made it to the table ... This salad was trendy for a while, but faded into insignificance, so in homage to that night I resurrect my version here, livened up with some crisp, sweet pear and crunchy, golden walnuts.

150 g (5½ oz/3⅓ cups) baby English spinach leaves
2 ripe but firm pears
2 teaspoons lemon juice
150 g (5½ oz) piece of pancetta
2½ tablespoons extra virgin olive oil
1 garlic clove, crushed
1½ tablespoons good-quality balsamic vinegar
1 teaspoon soft brown sugar
35 g (1¼ oz/⅓ cup) walnut halves, toasted & broken up

serves 4–6

Rinse the spinach leaves, then drain well in a colander or salad spinner. Cover and refrigerate until ready to serve. Slice the pears in half lengthways, remove the core using a sharp knife and slice the halves. Toss with the lemon juice and refrigerate.

Cut the pancetta into slices 5 mm (¼ inch) thick, then cut into short strips about 2½ cm (1 inch) long and 1 cm (½ inch) wide.

Heat 2 teaspoons of the extra virgin olive oil in a frying pan over medium–high heat. Add the pancetta and cook for 10 minutes, or until dark golden and crispy, stirring and turning occasionally. Remove with a slotted spoon and drain on paper towels.

Combine the remaining extra virgin olive oil, garlic, vinegar, sugar and 3 teaspoons water in a small bowl and whisk to make a smooth dressing. Season to taste.

In a bowl, gently toss together the spinach, pear, walnuts, pancetta and the dressing until well combined. Serve immediately.

spiced beetroot salad

Fresh beetroot is superb and just doesn't compare to the tinned stuff, which I find overly sweet. This dish is a great addition to a salad table, but also makes a lovely light lunch when you crumble some creamy goat's cheese over the top and serve it up with some crusty bread.

4 x 250 g (9 oz) beetroot (beets)
80 ml (2½ fl oz/⅓ cup) extra virgin olive oil
1½ tablespoons chardonnay vinegar or other
   white wine vinegar
1 tablespoon lemon juice
1½ teaspoons ground cumin
a pinch of ground allspice
2 garlic cloves, crushed
1 handful of coriander (cilantro) leaves, shredded
1 large handful of flat-leaf (Italian) parsley, shredded

serves 6–8

Trim each beetroot, leaving about 2 cm (¾ inch) of stem attached. Place in a large saucepan and cover well with water. Bring to the boil over high heat and cook for 1 hour, or until tender all the way through when pierced with the tip of a sharp knife. Remove from the heat and leave the beetroot in the cooking liquid to cool to room temperature. (Refrigerate the beetroot in the cooking liquid if you're not using it straight away.)

Meanwhile, make the dressing. Combine the extra virgin olive oil, vinegar, lemon juice, cumin, allspice and garlic in a small bowl and whisk together well. Stir in the herbs. Season to taste with salt and freshly ground black pepper and set aside for 20 minutes for the flavours to develop.

Drain and peel the beetroot and cut into wedges. Toss with the dressing and serve.

I get a little tired of heavy, mayonnaise-laden Dutch-style coleslaw which, after all, has been doing the rounds for over 200 years. In fact, it is believed that cabbage salads dressed with vinegar and eggs were being prepared as far back as ancient Roman times — now that's some testament to its popularity. The fresh, zippy Japanese-inspired dressing in this rendition has taken quite a leap from its roots, laced with soy sauce, sweet rice vinegar, ginger and sesame. It is refreshingly crisp and light, perfect for a steamy summer's day when traditional versions tend to — yick! — congeal.

asian coleslaw

1/4 green cabbage, finely sliced
1/4 red cabbage, finely sliced
3 spring onions (scallions), finely sliced
1 large celery stalk, finely chopped
1 large carrot, very finely julienned using a mandolin
   or very sharp knife
2 tablespoons light soy sauce
125 ml (4 fl oz/1/2 cup) rice vinegar
2 garlic cloves, crushed
1 1/2 teaspoons finely grated fresh ginger
45 g (1 3/4 oz/1/4 cup) soft brown sugar
2 1/2 teaspoons sesame oil
2 1/2 tablespoons full-flavoured peanut oil
2 1/2 tablespoons vegetable oil
30 g (1 oz/1/3 cup) toasted slivered or flaked almonds
2 tablespoons toasted sesame seeds

serves 6–8

Put all the cabbage in a large bowl with the spring onion, celery and carrot and toss well.

Put the soy sauce, rice vinegar, garlic, ginger and sugar in a small bowl with the sesame, peanut and vegetable oils. Whisk until the sugar has dissolved. Pour the dressing over the coleslaw and toss to coat well. Season to taste. Refrigerate for at least 1 hour, tossing now and then.

Just before serving, toss the toasted almonds and the sesame seeds through, reserving some for a garnish. Sprinkle the remaining almonds and sesame seeds over the top and serve immediately.

Every household has a favourite potato salad recipe. Sadly, for years you could only find it made with thick, sickly sweet bottled mayonnaise. Lighter options are the German-style potato salads, served warm with bacon and vinegar, or French style, served cold with a vinaigrette, but I'm a sucker for a creamy potato salad — as you'll see from this version, which has a definite Nordic slant, lifted by sharp and salty gherkins and capers, creamy horseradish and aromatic dill. Brilliant with barbecued seafood!

potato salad

1 kg (2 lb 4 oz) new or baby potatoes

185 ml (6 fl oz/³/₄ cup) whole-egg mayonnaise

310 g (11 oz/1¼ cups) sour cream

2 spring onions (scallions), finely sliced

1 celery stalk, finely diced

1½ tablespoons finely chopped dill, plus extra, to garnish

3 small, sweet, spiced gherkins (pickles), finely chopped

2 garlic cloves, crushed

2 tablespoons baby capers, rinsed & roughly chopped, plus extra whole baby capers, to garnish

2 tablespoons cider vinegar

2 tablespoons horseradish cream or relish

serves 6–8

Put the potatoes in a large saucepan, cover with cold water and bring to the boil over high heat. Cook for 10–12 minutes, or until tender all the way through when pierced with the tip of a sharp knife. Drain well and rinse with cold water, then allow to cool to room temperature. Cut the potatoes in half, unless they are very small, in which case leave them whole.

Meanwhile, combine the remaining ingredients in a bowl to make a dressing and season to taste.

Put the potatoes in a bowl and gently mix the dressing through. Garnish with the extra dill and a few extra capers and serve.

VARIATION: You can also add some crumbled, crispy bacon, or some sliced ham or smoked salmon.

green bean salad
with artichokes

If 'bean salad' conjures up images of slimy three-bean mix from a tin, you will no doubt be pleasantly surprised by this Mediterranean-style salad of lightly cooked, crisp baby green beans, mellow artichokes and rich olives, bound together with a light sherry vinegar dressing. I hope this helps erase all traumatic childhood bean-salad memories.

400 g (14 oz) baby green beans
6 whole artichoke hearts in olive oil, quartered
45 g (1¾ oz/¼ cup) ligurian olives (or other small
  black olives) in olive oil, drained

DRESSING
2 tablespoons good-quality sherry vinegar
60 ml (2 fl oz/¼ cup) extra virgin olive oil
1 tablespoon macadamia nut oil
1½ teaspoons dijon mustard
2½ teaspoons very finely chopped red onion
2 teaspoons soft brown sugar

serves 6

Bring a large saucepan of lightly salted water to the boil. Add the beans and cook for 5–6 minutes, or until just tender. Drain well, then plunge into a large bowl of iced water until cold. Drain well.

Put the dressing ingredients in a small bowl and whisk until smooth.

Combine the beans, artichoke and olives, then pour the dressing over and toss to coat well. Season to taste and serve.

VARIATION: Add 50 g (1¾ oz) thinly sliced prosciutto or some chunks of good-quality tuna to make this salad more substantial.

pasta salad

Another one of those salads that can evoke some scary emotions — but it can really be something special if you don't make it too far in advance, use fresh, flavoursome produce and keep it out of the sun until serving time. This pasta salad contains Italian, summery ingredients such as ripe tomatoes and basil, and is a fabulous accompaniment to grilled foods such as tuna, chicken, veal or lamb. It also happens to make a lovely light cold pasta main on its own.

180 g (6½ oz/2 cups) plain or wholemeal (whole-wheat) rigatoni or penne pasta

300 g (10½ oz) cherry tomatoes or baby roma (plum) tomatoes, cut in half

40 g (1½ oz/¼ cup) pine nuts, toasted

½ red onion, finely sliced

250 g (9 oz) cherry bocconcini (fresh baby mozzarella cheese)

1 handful of basil, torn, plus extra torn basil leaves, to garnish

50 g (1¾ oz/½ cup) finely grated good-quality parmesan cheese

DRESSING

80 ml (2½ fl oz/⅓ cup) extra virgin olive oil

2 tablespoons lemon juice

2 garlic cloves, crushed

1 handful of basil, very finely chopped

½ teaspoon caster (superfine) sugar

serves 6–8

Bring a large saucepan of salted water to the boil. Add the pasta and cook according to the packet instructions, or until *al dente*. Drain in a colander and rinse with cold running water.

Put all the dressing ingredients in a small bowl and whisk until smooth. Season to taste with salt and freshly cracked black pepper.

Put all the pasta salad ingredients in a serving bowl and gently toss together. Pour the dressing over and toss well. Season to taste, garnish with a few extra torn basil leaves and serve immediately.

❋ *Such sweet, fleshy pumpkin varieties are available these days that it seems a shame to only serve them up in a baked dinner. Jap pumpkin is especially flavoursome and absolutely delicious roasted. When cooled, it makes a fantastic salad for those warmer days, as in the recipe below.*

roast pumpkin
& rocket salad with creamy mustard dressing

1 small jap or kent pumpkin or 2 small butternut
   pumpkins (squash), about 2 kg (4 lb 8 oz)
   in total
60 ml (2 fl oz/¼ cup) olive oil
3 teaspoons sea salt flakes
a few large sprigs of thyme, broken into smaller sprigs
3 large handfuls of baby rocket (arugula)
50 g (1¾ oz/½ cup) walnuts, toasted &
   roughly chopped

CREAMY MUSTARD DRESSING
60 g (2¼ oz/¼ cup) wholegrain mustard
1 tablespoon lemon juice
1 tablespoon honey
2 teaspoons finely chopped thyme leaves
2 garlic cloves
1 tablespoon dry sherry
60 ml (2 fl oz/¼ cup) pouring (whipping) cream
125 g (4½ oz/½ cup) whole-egg mayonnaise

Preheat the oven to 220°C (425°F/Gas 7). Cut the pumpkin in half and remove the seeds, but do not peel. Cut into 2 cm (¾ inch) thick wedges or slices. Toss the pumpkin with the olive oil, sea salt flakes and thyme sprigs, then spread out in two roasting tins. Bake for 1 hour, or until the pumpkin is tender and well browned or caramelized on the edges. Remove from the oven and allow to cool to room temperature.

Put all the creamy mustard dressing ingredients in a bowl and whisk well. Refrigerate until ready to serve, then whisk again.

Lightly toss the pumpkin and rocket leaves in a bowl and gently tumble onto a serving platter. Drizzle with the dressing, sprinkle with the walnuts and serve.

serves 6–8

A barbecue for a bunch just isn't complete without a bowl of punch. Set up the punch bowl and let people serve themselves, but do post a warning: this one seems innocent enough, being so cooling and refreshing, but it does creep up on you — especially if you are sitting in the sun. They don't call it punch for nothing!

summer punch

1 small ripe honeydew melon
750 ml (26 fl oz/3 cups) cold black tea
1 litre (35 fl oz/4 cups) chilled pineapple juice
750 ml (26 fl oz/3 cups) chilled ginger ale
750 ml (26 fl oz/3 cups) white rum
500 ml (17 fl oz/2 cups) sherry
1 large handful of small mint leaves
1 starfruit, cut into 5 mm (¼ inch) slices
the pulp of 2 panama passionfruit, optional

**Makes 1 punch bowl
(about 4 litres/140 fl oz/16 cups)**

Use a melon baller to scoop out balls from the melon. Place on a lined baking tray, cover with plastic wrap, then freeze for 3 hours, or until hard. The melon balls will act as iceblocks in the punch to help keep it cool.

Combine the tea, pineapple juice, ginger ale, rum and sherry in a punch bowl. Roll the mint leaves a few at a time between your hands to bruise them, then add to the punch. Add the starfruit slices and passionfruit pulp, if using (you can strain it if you don't like the seeds). Add the frozen melon balls, stir and serve at once.

chapter three *with a CUPPA

MY GRANDPARENTS ARE NO LONGER WITH US BUT ONE OF MY FONDEST CHILDHOOD MEMORIES IS SHARING A CUP OF TEA WITH THEM — USUALLY ACCOMPANIED BY A PIECE OF HOME-MADE SLICE OR A BISCUIT. MY GRANDMOTHER WORKED AT A WELL-KNOWN SYDNEY CAKE SHOP IN HER YOUTH AND I LOVED IT WHEN SHE GAVE ME VALUABLE TIPS AND DEMONSTRATIONS ON ICING CAKES — WHICH OF COURSE HAD TO BE SAMPLED ON COMPLETION. WE HAVE A LARGE FAMILY AND IN THIS BUSY WORLD WE DON'T GET TO SEE EACH OTHER ENOUGH, BUT EVERY SO OFTEN I HOST AN AFTERNOON TEA FOR ALL THE LADIES — IT IS I SUPPOSE A RATHER OLD-FASHIONED THING TO DO, BUT I LOVE PREPARING BATCHES OF NAUGHTY THINGS THAT I RARELY COOK FOR MYSELF AND WATCHING FACES LIGHT UP AT THE SELECTION. SO MAYBE THERE ARE MORE GLASSES OF SPARKLING CONSUMED THAN CUPS OF TEA — BUT THE FOOD TASTES JUST AS GOOD!

* vanilla slice * pineapple upside-down cake with cardamom cream * nenish tarts * anzac biscuits * gingernut biscuits * scones with peach conserve & minted cream * date & nut loaf with butterscotch spread * lamingtons with white chocolate cream * carrot cake with orange cream cheese icing * chocolate cherry slice * chocolate crackles * jaffa cake * passionfruit sponge cake * orange, ginger & walnut shortbread * macadamia cake with lime syrup

✳ *I grew up near my Nana Doris and whenever I'd walk over to visit her, I'd inevitably stop off at the local cake shop for a couple of these delicious slices, in which vanilla custard is sandwiched between crisp puff pastry and either dusted with icing sugar, or glazed with a vanilla or passionfruit icing. Mmmmm. Although I am quite partial to the French-style vanilla slices available today with whipped cream folded through the custard, I felt this version had to be what most of us remember!*

vanilla slice

2 sheets of ready-made puff pastry
icing (confectioners') sugar, for sprinkling, or
    passionfruit icing (frosting) (see page 112),
    for topping

VANILLA CUSTARD
115 g (4 oz/1/2 cup) caster (superfine) sugar
90 g (3¼ oz/¾ cup) vanilla custard powder
    (instant vanilla pudding mix)
3 teaspoons cornflour (cornstarch)
500 ml (17 fl oz/2 cups) milk
375 ml (13 fl oz/1½ cups) pouring (whipping) cream
3 large egg yolks, lightly beaten
50 g (1¾ oz) unsalted butter, diced
1½ teaspoons natural vanilla extract

serves 6–8

Preheat the oven to 220°C (425°F/Gas 7). Place each pastry sheet on a lightly greased baking tray, prick all over with a fork, then sit a baking tray on top of each to weigh them down slightly — this will help the pastry rise evenly. Bake for 25 minutes, or until deep golden all over. Allow to cool completely on wire racks, then trim the pastry to fit a deep, 22 cm (8½ inch) square cake tin.

Meanwhile, make the vanilla custard. Combine the sugar, custard powder, cornflour and 80 ml (2½ fl oz/1/3 cup) of the milk in a saucepan and whisk until smooth. Place over medium–high heat and stir continuously while gradually whisking in the remaining milk and the cream. Stir continuously until the mixture boils and thickens, then reduce the heat and simmer for 5 minutes. Remove from the heat and whisk in the egg yolks, butter and vanilla, then return to the heat and stir for a further 2–3 minutes, or until the egg is just cooked through and does not taste raw.

To assemble, line the base of the cake tin with a long strip of baking paper so that it overhangs on two sides — this will help to lift out the slice. Fit a layer of pastry in the base of the tin. Dollop the vanilla custard over the top and smooth over. Top with the second layer of pastry, turned upside down so the flattest side is facing up. Press down slightly and refrigerate until firm.

To serve, generously sift icing sugar over the top, or spread with passionfruit icing and allow to set. The custard in this slice is still quite soft, so use a serrated knife and a light sawing action to cut it into six or eight rectangles before serving.

I first learned how to cook this cake at a local cooking school when I was about 12. I have to admit I hadn't cooked it much in the years since, although my memory of it was always fond. While developing this recipe I rediscovered the joy of this simple cake topped with sunshine in a tin — it's definitely back on the favourites list.

* pineapple
upside-down cake
with cardamom cream

100 g (3¹/₂ oz) unsalted butter

125 g (4¹/₂ oz/²/₃ cup) soft brown sugar

90 g (3¹/₄ oz/¹/₄ cup) golden syrup (if unavailable,
  substitute with half honey & half dark corn syrup)

2 x 440 g (15¹/₂ oz) tins of pineapple rings in
  unsweetened juice (reserve the juice)

CAKE

125 g (4¹/₂ oz) unsalted butter, softened

170 g (6 oz/³/₄ cup) caster (superfine) sugar

3 large eggs, at room temperature

185 g (6¹/₂ oz/1¹/₂ cups) self-raising flour, sifted

80 g (2³/₄ oz/³/₄ cup) ground almonds or
  macadamia nuts

45 g (1³/₄ oz/¹/₂ cup) desiccated coconut

¹/₄ teaspoon ground cardamom

160 g (5³/₄ oz/²/₃ cup) sour cream

1 teaspoon natural vanilla extract

80 ml (2¹/₂ fl oz/¹/₃ cup) reserved pineapple juice

CARDAMOM CREAM

310 ml (10³/₄ fl oz/1¹/₄ cups) pouring (whipping) cream

30 g (1 oz/¹/₄ cup) icing (confectioners') sugar, sifted

¹/₄ teaspoon ground cardamom

serves 8

Preheat the oven to 180°C (350°F/Gas 4). Put the butter, brown sugar and golden syrup in a small saucepan and stir over medium heat until the butter has melted. Pour into a lightly greased 22 cm (8¹/₂ inch) square cake tin — do not use a non-stick tin as it will prevent the sugar caramelizing properly.

Drain the tinned pineapple, reserving 80 ml (2¹/₂ fl oz/¹/₃ cup) of the juice for the cake batter. Cut each pineapple ring into three even pieces then, starting at the outside edge of the cake tin, place them in neat rows over the base. You will have a few pieces left over.

To make the cake, beat the butter and sugar using electric beaters until pale and creamy. Beat in the eggs one at a time until well incorporated. Combine the flour, ground almonds, coconut and cardamom. Combine the sour cream and vanilla. With the motor on low speed, mix half the flour mixture into the creamed butter until combined, then half the sour cream mixture until combined. Now mix in the pineapple juice — the mixture will appear slightly curdled. Mix in the remaining flour mixture, then the remaining sour cream mixture, until well combined.

Carefully spoon the cake batter over the pineapple pieces, being careful not to disturb the pattern. Smooth the batter and lightly tap the base of the tin on the bench to eliminate any air bubbles.

Bake on the middle shelf of the oven for 40–45 minutes, or until a skewer inserted in the centre comes out clean. Run a small knife around the inside edge of the tin, then invert the cake onto a serving plate but leave the tin on top for 5 minutes to help the topping to settle.

Meanwhile, combine all the cardamom cream ingredients in a chilled bowl and whip until light and fluffy. Cover and refrigerate until ready to serve.

Carefully remove the tin from the cake and replace any pieces of pineapple that may have stuck to it. Serve the cake warm or at room temperature with a dollop of cardamom cream.

These tiny tarts are usually filled with a vanilla-flavoured mock cream, an inferior substitute for fresh cream. In researching the authentic filling it became clear that the origin of nenish, neenish or nienich tarts is in fact highly dubious. I finally settled on developing a recipe in keeping with my memory of after-school treats, combined with how I would like them to taste today, using an almond pastry, fresh cream and real chocolate.

nenish tarts

PASTRY

125 g (4¹/2 oz) unsalted butter, chilled & diced
60 g (2¹/4 oz/¹/2 cup) icing (confectioners') sugar, sifted
185 g (6¹/2 oz/1¹/2 cups) plain (all-purpose) flour, sifted
80 g (2³/4 oz/³/4 cup) ground almonds
1 egg, lightly beaten

FILLING

185 ml (6 fl oz/³/4 cup) pouring (whipping) cream
30 g (1 oz/¹/4 cup) icing (confectioners') sugar, sifted
1¹/2 teaspoons of natural vanilla extract, sherry or rum
2 tablespoons strawberry, raspberry or cherry jam, optional

VANILLA ICING (FROSTING)

185 g (6¹/2 oz/1¹/2 cups) icing (confectioners') sugar, sifted
1 teaspoon natural vanilla extract
1¹/2 tablespoons boiling water
50 g (1³/4 oz) good-quality dark chocolate

makes 16

Lightly grease 16 patty pan or mini muffin tin holes measuring 7 cm (2³/4 inches) across the top, 4 cm (1¹/2 inches) across the base and 2.5 cm (1 inch) deep, with sides sloping outwards. Smaller tins will give more tarts, but will hold less filling and may be too sweet.

To make the pastry, put the butter, icing sugar, flour and ground almonds in a food processor and pulse until the mixture resembles breadcrumbs. Add the egg and pulse until it just comes together. (Alternatively, rub the butter, icing sugar and flour together using your fingers until breadcrumbs form. Stir in the almonds, then the egg, until it just comes together.) If the pastry is still a little dry, add some chilled water, just a teaspoon at a time, until it comes together. Gather together, wrap in plastic wrap and refrigerate for 30 minutes.

Roll the pastry out between two pieces of baking paper to an even 2–3 mm (¹/16–¹/8 inch) thickness. Remove the top layer of paper and cut out pastry rounds with a 10 cm (4 inch) circular biscuit (cookie) cutter. Press the pastry discs into the bases of the muffin holes. Prick the bases with a fork, then refrigerate for 30 minutes.

Meanwhile, preheat the oven to 180°C (350°F/Gas 4). Bake the pastry cases for 10–15 minutes, or until lightly golden. Allow to cool in the tins on a wire rack. Remove just prior to filling.

To make the filling, whisk the cream, icing sugar and vanilla together until firmly whipped. Refrigerate until ready to use.

To assemble, put a quarter teaspoon of jam, if using, in each tart case. Spread with 1¹/2–2 tablespoons of the whipped cream so it is smooth and just below the top of the pastry. Chill for 30 minutes.

To make the vanilla icing, put the icing sugar, vanilla and boiling water in a bowl and mix until smooth but quite thick. Spread over the tarts in one smooth, circular movement. Chill again to set.

Meanwhile, very gently melt the chocolate in a heatproof bowl over a saucepan of simmering water, stirring until smooth. When cooled to room temperature, neatly spread the chocolate over one half of the vanilla icing. Refrigerate until the chocolate has set, then serve.

✳ with a cuppa [page 093]

*These crispy biscuits, apparently adapted from a Scottish oatcake recipe,
are believed to have originally been shipped in airtight 'billy tea' tins to
Australian troops in Gallipoli during World War I as the women at home began
to worry about the lack of nutritious foods their men were receiving. So the
biscuits wouldn't spoil on the long journey, eggs were omitted — a good thing as
they were scarce anyway. Instead, the mixture was bound by golden syrup!*

anzac biscuits

100 g (3$\frac{1}{2}$ oz/1 cup) rolled (porridge) oats
170 g (6 oz/$\frac{3}{4}$ cup) caster (superfine) sugar
60 g (2$\frac{1}{4}$ oz/$\frac{2}{3}$ cup) desiccated coconut
125 g (4$\frac{1}{2}$ oz/1 cup) plain (all-purpose) flour
1 teaspoon ground ginger
125 g (4$\frac{1}{2}$ oz) unsalted butter
90 g (3$\frac{1}{4}$ oz/$\frac{1}{4}$ cup) golden syrup (if unavailable,
    substitute with half honey & half dark corn syrup)
1 teaspoon bicarbonate of soda (baking soda)

makes about 24

Preheat the oven to 160°C (315°F/Gas 2–3). Lightly grease two baking trays or line with baking paper.

Put the rolled oats, sugar and coconut in a bowl. Sift the flour and ginger into the bowl, then mix thoroughly to combine. Make a well in the centre.

Melt the butter and golden syrup together, then pour into the well. Dissolve the bicarbonate of soda in 1 tablespoon of boiling water and add to the bowl. Mix well, then take tablespoons of the mixture and roll into balls. Place well apart on the baking trays to allow for spreading, press down on each to flatten slightly, then bake for 15 minutes, or until crisp and golden. Allow to cool briefly on the trays, then carefully remove the biscuits and leave to cool completely on wire racks.

VARIATIONS: Here are a few flavour variations, but note that the plain mixture spreads more easily and will be a little more crispy. Before stirring in the melted butter mixture, you could add 3 tablespoons of one of the following: dark chocolate chips, or chopped nuts of your choice (e.g. peanuts, almonds, walnuts, macadamias), or finely chopped dates, glacé ginger, glacé cherries, or dried or glacé apricots.

gingernut biscuits

There is more than one way to crack a nut — a gingernut, that is. Although originally an English recipe, gingernut biscuits are so popular in Australia that one major biscuit manufacturer bakes no less than four separate varieties in four different states. No matter whether you prefer them light or dark, thick or thin, firm or rock-hard, everyone agrees they should be dunked in a cuppa before consuming (less risk to your teeth or dentures). Here's hoping these gingernuts will satisfy a cross-section of die-hard fans, or it's back to the drawing board for me ...

150 g (5½ oz) unsalted butter, softened
125 g (4½ oz/⅔ cup) soft brown sugar
235 g (8½ oz/⅔ cup) treacle or molasses
250 g (9 oz/2 cups) plain (all-purpose) flour
1 tablespoon ground ginger
½ teaspoon mixed (pumpkin pie) spice
¼ teaspoon bicarbonate of soda (baking soda)

makes 24

Beat the butter and sugar using electric beaters until pale and creamy. With the beaters still running, gradually add the treacle and beat until well combined. Sift together the flour, ginger, mixed spice and bicarbonate of soda, then stir into the treacle mixture until well combined — you should have a thick paste. Refrigerate for 2 hours.

Preheat the oven to 170°C (325°F/Gas 3). Roll level tablespoons of the mixture into balls and place on lightly greased baking trays, spaced apart to allow for spreading. Press down to flatten slightly, then bake for 22 minutes, or until golden and dry to the touch. (If you prefer a crispier biscuit, bake for up to 3 minutes longer.)

Remove from the oven and allow to cool on the tray for a few minutes, then transfer to a wire rack to cool completely.

with a cuppa [page 095]

lamingtons with white chocolate cream &
scones with peach conserve & minted cream

scones with peach conserve & minted cream

PEACH CONSERVE

600 g (1 lb 5 oz) ripe peaches
230 g (8½ oz/1 cup) caster (superfine) sugar
½ teaspoon finely grated fresh ginger
½ vanilla bean, split lengthways
½ teaspoon finely grated orange zest
2 tablespoons orange juice

MINTED CREAM

310 ml (10¾ fl oz/1¼ cups) pouring (whipping) cream
1½ tablespoons icing (confectioners') sugar
1 tablespoon finely chopped mint

SCONES

500 g (1 lb 2 oz/4 cups) self-raising flour
2 tablespoons icing (confectioners') sugar
50 g (1¾ oz) unsalted butter, melted
375–435 ml (13–15¼ fl oz/1½–1¾ cups) pouring
   (whipping) cream, plus extra, for glazing

makes 16 scones

First, make the peach conserve. Remove the stones from the peaches and tie them in a small piece of muslin (cheesecloth). Cut the peaches into 2 cm (¾ inch) dice and put them in a saucepan with the sugar. Leave for 20 minutes to allow the juices to leach out.

Add the peach stones to the pan (they will add flavour to the jam) with the ginger, vanilla bean, orange zest and orange juice. Stir occasionally over high heat until the liquid comes to the boil. Reduce the heat and simmer for 30 minutes, or until the peaches and liquid are darker, and the liquid has a slight gel-like consistency. Pour into a very clean 375 ml (13 fl oz/1½ cup) jar, discarding the peach stones, and seal. Allow to cool to room temperature, then refrigerate until needed.

To make the minted cream, whip the cream with the icing sugar until firm peaks form. Stir in the mint and refrigerate until needed.

Preheat the oven to 220°C (425°F/Gas 7). To make the scones, sift the flour, icing sugar and a large pinch of salt into a bowl and make a well in the centre. Pour in the melted butter and 1½ cups of the cream, then use a flat-bladed knife to quickly mix together to form soft, doughy clumps. Use the remaining cream if necessary. The moisture content of the flour can be affected by weather and therefore you sometimes need to add a little more liquid. Turn out onto a lightly floured work surface and gently knead, just to bring the mixture together. Gently roll or press the dough out evenly until 1.5 cm (⅝ inch) thick. Use a 6 cm (2½ inch) round cutter to cut out the scones — do not drag or twist the cutter, just cut straight down in one sharp movement and up again.

Put the scones on a lightly greased baking tray, close together so they will help push each other up. Lightly brush the tops with a little cream, being careful not to let it drip down the sides, as this will hinder the rising process. Bake for about 10 minutes, or until the scones are puffed and the tops lightly golden. Gently pat any leftover dough together and cut out and bake more scones — unfortunately they won't be as light as the first batch.

While the scones are baking, take the peach conserve out of the fridge to warm up a little. Allow the scones to cool slightly, then split them in half and serve with the peach conserve and mint cream.

Although my friends find it hard to believe, I was once a Brownie! As it happens, my first memory of making scones was in Brown Owl's tiny kitchen where, on completion of several dozen rough-looking mounds, I was awarded my cooking badge. Who knew where that would lead? These simple quickbreads, a Scottish invention, were traditionally made with oats and were no doubt sturdier in texture than the style popular today. This recipe is oh so easy — but remember that a very light touch is needed to make the finest scones: overmixing or kneading will lead to dense, heavy, inedible blobs. Good scones will pull apart with ease, and are best served warm or just upon cooling. The minted cream and peach conserve are wonderful when peaches are in season, but jam and butter or whipped cream are perfect accompaniments anytime.
Brown Owl says so!

This is a dressed-up version of a simple date and nut loaf — something I remember eating at a friend's place after school as a semi-healthy snack. On cold, rainy afternoons it was usually toasted with a smear of butter melting into each slice. If you happen to have any leftovers it's handy to know that the luscious dates make this loaf moist, helping it to keep well — I also recommend freezing it in portions for popping in the toaster for a quick breakfast or anytime-treat. The butterscotch spread makes this old favourite a little more decadent than you may remember it, and of course is optional.

date & nut loaf
with butterscotch spread

BUTTERSCOTCH SPREAD

20 g (³/₄ oz) unsalted butter

45 g (1³/₄ oz/¹/₄ cup) soft brown sugar

2 tablespoons golden syrup (if unavailable, substitute
with half honey & half dark corn syrup)

¹/₂ teaspoon natural vanilla extract

125 g (4¹/₂ oz/¹/₂ cup) cream cheese, softened

DATE LOAF

300 g (10¹/₂ oz/1²/₃ cups) pitted dates, chopped

185 ml (6 fl oz/³/₄ cup) milk

¹/₂ teaspoon bicarbonate of soda (baking soda)

250 g (9 oz) unsalted butter, softened & chopped

125 g (4¹/₂ oz/²/₃ cup) soft brown sugar

115 g (4 oz/¹/₃ cup) golden syrup (if unavailable,
substitute with half honey & half dark corn syrup)

3 eggs

250 g (9 oz/2 cups) self-raising flour, sifted

3 teaspoons mixed (pumpkin pie) spice

85 g (3 oz/²/₃ cup) roughly chopped walnuts

makes 1 loaf (serves 8)

To make the butterscotch spread, put the butter, sugar, golden syrup and vanilla in a small saucepan over medium heat. Stir until the mixture comes to the boil, then reduce the heat and simmer over very low heat for 4 minutes, or until thickened slightly, stirring occasionally. Remove from the heat and allow to cool completely. Beat the cream cheese using electric beaters for 10 minutes, or until very smooth. Gradually beat in the cooled butterscotch mixture until completely smooth. Refrigerate until firm enough to spread.

Preheat the oven to 160°C (315°F/Gas 2–3). Grease a loaf (bar) tin measuring 22 x 9 cm (8¹/₂ x 3¹/₂ inches) and 9 cm (3¹/₂ inches) deep. Line the base with baking paper.

To make the date loaf, put the dates and milk in a small saucepan and bring just to the boil. Remove from the heat and stir in the bicarbonate of soda until dissolved. Allow to cool to room temperature.

Beat the butter, sugar and golden syrup using electric beaters until pale and creamy. Beat in the eggs, one at a time, beating well after each addition. Stir in the date mixture, then stir in the flour, mixed spice and walnuts and mix thoroughly. Pour into the prepared tin and smooth the surface, then make a furrow down the centre, along the length of the cake — this will stop the loaf from peaking too much in the centre.

Bake for 1¹/₄ hours, or until a skewer comes out clean when inserted in the centre of the loaf. Note that it will look quite dark. Allow the loaf to cool in the tin for 5 minutes, before inverting onto a wire rack to cool slightly. Serve warm, at room temperature, or toasted, with the butterscotch spread on the side.

✳ lamingtons with white chocolate cream

CAKE

4 large eggs, at room temperature
145 g (5$^{1}/_2$ oz/$^{2}/_3$ cup) caster (superfine) sugar
125 ml (4 fl oz/$^{1}/_2$ cup) milk
60 g (2$^{1}/_4$ oz) unsalted butter
185 g (6$^{1}/_2$ oz/1$^{1}/_2$ cups) self-raising flour
30 g (1 oz/$^{1}/_4$ cup) cornflour (cornstarch)
1 teaspoon cream of tartar

WHITE CHOCOLATE CREAM

310 ml (10$^{3}/_4$ fl oz/1$^{1}/_4$ cups) pouring (whipping) cream
100 g (3$^{1}/_2$ oz) good-quality white chocolate, chopped

CHOCOLATE ICING (FROSTING)

310 g (11 oz/2$^{1}/_2$ cups) icing (confectioners')
   sugar, sifted
40 g (1$^{1}/_2$ oz/$^{1}/_3$ cup) good-quality unsweetened
   cocoa powder
50 g (1$^{3}/_4$ oz) unsalted butter
80 ml (2$^{1}/_2$ fl oz/$^{1}/_3$ cup) milk

270 g (9$^{1}/_2$ oz/3 cups) desiccated coconut

makes 16

Make the cake a day ahead as it will be less delicate and crumbly and will be easier to ice.

Preheat the oven to 180°C (350°F/Gas 4). Grease a rectangular cake tin measuring 20 x 30 cm (8 x 12 inches) and 4 cm (1$^{1}/_2$ inches) deep, and line the base with baking paper. Beat the eggs using electric beaters on high for 5 minutes, or until the mixture is thick and creamy and holds a trail when the beaters are lifted. With the beaters still running, gradually add the sugar and continue mixing until the sugar has dissolved.

Meanwhile, gently heat the milk and butter until the butter has melted. Sift the flour, cornflour and cream of tartar together. Fold half the flour mixture into the egg mixture, then mix in half the milk mixture. Repeat with the remaining flour and milk, mixing until well combined. Pour the batter into the prepared tin and bake for 20 minutes, or until golden on top and firm to the touch. Allow to stand in the tin on a wire rack for 5 minutes, before inverting onto the rack to cool completely. Wrap in plastic wrap and refrigerate overnight.

The next day, make the white chocolate cream. Gently heat the cream and chocolate in a small saucepan over low heat until the chocolate has just melted, stirring well. Allow the mixture to cool slightly, then cover and refrigerate. When cold, whip until firm peaks form, but do not overbeat or the mixture will split.

Combine the chocolate icing ingredients in a large saucepan and stir over medium heat until the butter has melted and the mixture is smooth and runny. Place about a quarter of the coconut on a plate.

Trim the very edges of the cooled cake to neaten, then cut into rectangles measuring 4 x 7 cm (1$^{1}/_2$ x 2$^{3}/_4$ inches) — you will end up with 16 rectangles. Dip the cake rectangles into the chocolate icing, turn to cover completely, and allow the excess to drip back into the saucepan. Immediately press each side into the coconut, then place on a wire rack until the icing has set. Add more coconut to the plate as you need it.

When the icing has set, carefully cut each cake all the way through the middle with a serrated knife. Pipe or spoon some white chocolate cream onto one of the cut surfaces, then sandwich the halves back together. Serve immediately, or refrigerate until ready to serve.

As with the pavlova, Australians and New Zealanders proudly call lamingtons their own, and enjoy a friendly rivalry over both of these antipodean food icons. There is a strong belief among Australians that these chocolate and coconut-coated cakes were named after Lord Lamington, a Queensland Governor in the late 1800s. Several different versions of the story suggest it was developed quite by accident in the kitchen of the Governor's abode. Well, whatever the case, here is my version — the filling might be a little fancy for your local school fete, but your friends and family won't mind.

Carrots are an old-world vegetable and as such have been used in all manner of recipes throughout the ages, with the first written reference to a type of pudding or cake being recorded in medieval times. Carrot cake, a particular favourite of the Swiss, enjoyed a resurgence in the UK, US and Australia around the 1930s and then again in the 1970s, although this time it was marketed as a healthy alternative to other less nutritious baked goods and desserts. In the early 1980s I worked for a short time as a sales assistant in a 'too quiet for me' clothing store where my daydreams often featured food — the highlight of my working day being the pineapple-studded carrot cake with lemony cream cheese icing that I would savour almost every lunchtime. It was divinely moist yet light, and was of course my inspiration for this recipe.

carrot cake with orange cream cheese icing

310 g (11 oz/2½ cups) self-raising flour
3 teaspoons ground cinnamon
280 g (10 oz/1½ cups) soft brown sugar
3 large carrots, grated
250 g (9 oz/1 cup) sour cream
125 ml (4 fl oz/½ cup) vegetable oil
4 large eggs
1 teaspoon natural vanilla extract
3 teaspoons finely grated orange zest
175 g (6 oz/⅔ cup) drained, tinned crushed pineapple
60 g (2¼ oz/about ½ cup) walnuts, pecans or
    macadamia nuts, chopped

ORANGE CREAM CHEESE ICING (FROSTING)

250 g (9 oz/1 cup) cream cheese
210 g (7½ oz/1⅔ cups) icing (confectioners')
    sugar, sifted
1½ teaspoons natural vanilla extract
1½ teaspoons finely grated orange zest
1½ tablespoons strained, freshly squeezed
    orange juice
roughly chopped walnuts, to decorate, optional

serves 8

Preheat the oven to 160°C (315°F/Gas 2–3). Lightly grease a deep, 22 cm (8½ inch) non-stick square or round cake tin and line the base with baking paper.

Sift the flour and cinnamon into a large bowl. Add the sugar and grated carrot and toss until well combined. Beat together the sour cream, vegetable oil, eggs, vanilla and orange zest until smooth, then mix into the carrot mixture. Stir in the pineapple and nuts. Pour the mixture into the prepared tin. Bake for 50–55 minutes, or until a skewer inserted into the centre of the cake comes out clean. Allow the cake to cool in the tin on a wire rack for 10 minutes, before inverting onto a wire rack to cool completely.

To make the orange cream cheese icing, beat the cream cheese, icing sugar, vanilla, orange zest and orange juice using electric beaters for 10 minutes, or until very smooth. Evenly spread the icing over the top of the cooled cake. Decorate the top with chopped walnuts, if desired.

✳ with a cuppa [page 105]

chocolate cherry slice

Inspired by a popular Australian confectionery bar, this sweet slice combines a layer of glacé cherries and coconut over a chocolate biscuit base, beneath a layer of rich, smooth, dark chocolate. Cherry Ripe bars have been around in Australia since 1924 and are still a best-selling chocolate. They were a favourite of my mum's at one stage and I inherited her addiction, but I have managed to cut back now. This slice is a great way to share an exquisite treat with friends.

BISCUIT (COOKIE) BASE

155 g (5¾ oz/1¼ cups) plain (all-purpose) flour
60 g (2¼ oz/⅓ cup) soft brown sugar
2 tablespoons unsweetened cocoa powder
125 g (4½ oz) unsalted butter, melted
1 teaspoon natural vanilla extract

365 g (13 oz/1¾ cups) red glacé cherries,
    finely chopped
90 g (3¼ oz/½ cup) dried sour cherries,
    finely chopped
135 g (4¾ oz/1½ cups) desiccated coconut
315 ml (10¾ fl oz/1 cup) sweetened condensed milk
1 tablespoon cherry liqueur or kirsch, optional
80 g (2¾ oz) Copha (white vegetable shortening),
    melted
250 g (9 oz) good-quality dark chocolate

Makes about 20 pieces

Preheat the oven to 180°C (350°F/Gas 4). Line a 28 x 20 cm (11¼ x 8 inch) slice tin (one about 4 cm/1½ inches deep) with baking paper so that it overhangs the two long edges.

To make the biscuit base, combine the flour, sugar and cocoa powder, then stir the melted butter and vanilla through until the mixture comes together. Press the mixture evenly into the base of the lined tin, prick all over with a fork, then bake for 20–25 minutes, or until dry to the touch. Remove from the oven and allow to cool.

Combine the glacé and dried cherries, coconut, condensed milk, liqueur if using, and melted Copha, then spread evenly over the cooled base. Refrigerate until firm.

Chop the chocolate into even-sized pieces. Place in a heatproof bowl over a saucepan of simmering water, ensuring the water doesn't touch the base of the bowl, and stir occasionally until just melted. Remove the bowl from the pan and stir until smooth. Pour the chocolate over the cherry filling and spread out evenly to cover. Refrigerate until the chocolate is firm.

Lift the slice from the tin using the overhanging baking paper, and cut into small fingers to serve.

chocolate crackles

This crunchy, chocolatey treat has been a staple at every kids' birthday party since I can remember — the not so secret ingredient, Rice Bubbles, a puffed rice cereal, being introduced to supermarket shelves as far back as 1929. Big kids and little kids love them, and I suspect children's parties are really just an excuse for adults to make them. My dear friend Vanessa advises against letting kids have them at all after an incident when she flopped into bed, exhausted from a function for very small people, only to find chocolate crackles crunched and smeared all over her clean sheets! Here is my take on the original recipe, using real chocolate — which may just make them even more of a hit with the adults, so you might want to whip up a double batch if you have to share them with the littlies.

37 g (1¼ oz/1¼ cups) puffed rice cereal

40 g (1½ oz/⅓ cup) icing (confectioners') sugar, sifted

45 g (1¾ oz/½ cup) desiccated coconut, lightly toasted

1 heaped teaspoon good-quality unsweetened cocoa powder

150 g (5½ oz) good-quality dark chocolate

makes 24 small crackles

Put the puffed rice, icing sugar, coconut and cocoa powder in a bowl and mix together well.

Chop the chocolate into even-sized pieces. Place in a heatproof bowl over a saucepan of simmering water, ensuring the water doesn't touch the base of the bowl, and stir occasionally until just melted. Remove the bowl from the pan and stir until smooth.

Pour the chocolate into the puffed rice mixture and stir until all the ingredients are thoroughly combined. Spoon into 24 small paper cases and refrigerate until firm. (If you can wait that long!)

VARIATIONS: Make rocky road chocolate crackles by adding some finely chopped glacé cherries, macadamia nuts and marshmallows — or try substituting white chocolate for dark, omitting the cocoa powder and adding some finely chopped Turkish delight, pistachio nuts and dried or glacé apricots.

❋ jaffa cake &
chocolate cherry slice

jaffa cake

ORANGE CAKE

150 g (5½ oz) unsalted butter, chopped & softened
230 g (8½ oz/1 cup) caster (superfine) sugar
3 large eggs, at room temperature
3 teaspoons finely grated orange zest
60 ml (2 fl oz/¼ cup) freshly squeezed orange juice
1 teaspoon natural vanilla extract
210 g (7½ oz/1⅔ cups) self-raising flour
155 g (5¾ oz/1½ cups) ground almonds
185 ml (6 fl oz/¾ cup) milk

MARMALADE BUTTERCREAM

150 g (5½ oz) unsalted butter, chopped & softened
2 tablespoons pouring (whipping) cream
1 teaspoon natural vanilla extract
125 g (4½ oz/1 cup) icing (confectioners') sugar
105 g (3¾ oz/⅓ cup) good-quality orange marmalade

DARK CHOCOLATE GLAZE

200 g (7 oz) good-quality dark chocolate
50 g (1¾ oz) unsalted butter
30 g (1 oz/¼ cup) icing (confectioners') sugar, sifted
1½ tablespoons pouring (whipping) cream

serves 8–10

Preheat the oven to 180°C (350°F/Gas 4). Grease a deep, non-stick, 20 cm (8 inch) round cake tin and line the base with baking paper.

To make the orange cake, beat the butter and sugar using electric beaters until pale and creamy. Beat in the eggs, one at a time, mixing well after each addition. Beat in the orange zest, orange juice and vanilla. Mix in half the flour and ground almonds, then half the milk. Repeat with the remaining flour, almonds and milk. Pour into the prepared cake tin and bake for 50–60 minutes, or until a skewer inserted into the centre of the cake comes out clean and the top is firm to the touch. Remove from the oven and leave in the tin for 10 minutes, before inverting onto a cake rack to cool completely.

Meanwhile, to make the marmalade buttercream, beat the butter using electric beaters until pale and creamy. Combine the cream and vanilla. Gradually beat the icing sugar and cream mixture alternately into the butter until smooth and fluffy. Beat in the marmalade.

Cut the cooled cake in half through the middle. Evenly spread the bottom half with the marmalade buttercream. Place the top half back on, to sandwich the cake together.

To make the dark chocolate glaze, put the chocolate, butter, icing sugar and cream in a small saucepan over low heat. Stir until smooth and glossy.

Pour the glaze on top of the cake, then smoothly spread over the top and sides using a metal spatula or flat-bladed knife dipped in hot water. Allow the glaze to set. Serve immediately, or refrigerate until ready to serve, bringing the cake to room temperature just before serving.

Rich with dark chocolate, orange and almonds, this dense, moist cake is a sweet reminder of those orange candy-coated chocolate balls we all loved as kids (some of us still do). In Australia, back when movie cinemas still had wooden floorboards, kids would roll Jaffas down the aisles while the film was screening, revelling in the racket they made. Well you can't quite roll this cake down the aisle, but why would you want to waste good chocolate anyway? Jaffas are named after the sweet jaffa orange, but the word 'jaffa' is now also generally used to describe the combination of chocolate–orange flavours. And if you are a fan of all things jaffa you will know only too well the fabulous English jaffa cake biscuits filled with an addictive orange jelly! If you can bear to wait longer than it takes to rip open a packet of biscuits, give this very special cake a try.

❋ *My local department-store cafeteria never takes passionfruit sponge cake off the menu. Although my Aunty Ruth always hungrily eyes it off, she only orders herself a slice as a special treat and I love watching her savour every mouthful. This version is rather special — and gets my aunt's expert nod of approval.*

passionfruit
sponge cake

PASSIONFRUIT CURD

3 teaspoons lemon juice

80 ml (2½ fl oz/⅓ cup) passionfruit pulp

2 large eggs, lightly beaten

1 large egg yolk, lightly beaten

75 g (2¾ oz) unsalted butter, chilled & diced

80 g (2¾ oz/⅓ cup) caster (superfine) sugar

SPONGE CAKE

4 large eggs

170 g (6 oz/¾ cup) caster (superfine) sugar

½ teaspoon natural vanilla extract

60 g (2¼ oz/½ cup) cornflour (cornstarch)

60 g (2¼ oz/½ cup) self-raising flour

PASSIONFRUIT ICING (FROSTING)

125 g (4½ oz/1 cup) icing (confectioners') sugar, sifted

20 g (¾ oz) butter, softened

2 tablespoons passionfruit pulp

250 ml (9 fl oz/1 cup) pouring (whipping) cream, whipped & kept chilled

serves 6

Put the passionfruit curd ingredients in a heatproof bowl and stir continuously over a saucepan of simmering water for 30 minutes, or until the curd is glossy, easily coats the back of a spoon, and holds a trail when you run a finger through it. Strain and cool slightly, then refrigerate for 3 hours, or until completely cold and thickened.

Preheat the oven to 180°C (350°F/Gas 4). Lightly grease two deep, round 20 cm (8 inch) cake tins and line the bases with baking paper.

To make the sponge cake, beat the eggs, sugar and vanilla using electric beaters on high for 10 minutes, or until all the sugar has dissolved and the mixture is pale and creamy. It should hold a 'ribbon' shape when drizzled from the beaters back into the bowl. Combine the cornflour and flour, then sift three times to ensure it is well aerated. Sift the flours over the top of the egg mixture and gently but quickly fold into the mixture until just combined. Be careful not to overmix or you will beat out the air.

Carefully divide the batter between the two prepared tins. Bake, without opening the oven door, for 20 minutes, or until the cakes are well risen and browned on top and have slightly shrunk away from the edge of the tins. Cool in the tins on a wire rack for 5 minutes, then turn out onto the wire rack to cool completely.

To make the passionfruit icing, combine the icing sugar, butter and 1½ tablespoons of the passionfruit pulp and stir until smooth. If needed, add the remaining pulp, a teaspoon at a time, until the icing is of a smooth, flowing consistency.

Ice (frost) the bottom or flat side of one of the sponge cakes — you can let it run down the sides a little if you like — then leave until the icing has set. When ready to serve, spread the other sponge cake with the passionfruit curd, then top with the whipped cream. Place the iced cake on top and serve immediately.

NOTE: The passionfruit icing is very sweet — leave it off if you prefer and dust the top with sifted icing sugar before serving.

We have the dairy farmers of medieval Scotland to thank in part for these tempting morsels. The availability of butter as a cooking fat way back then made it a popular addition to foods, one of the most famous being of course Scottish shortbread — butter being one of the three main ingredients, together with flour (originally oats) and sugar. Shortening is the name given to a fat that is added to a dough to make it more crumbly and melt-in-the-mouth. The more shortening used, the more 'short' or tender and crumbly a product becomes.

The original large, sun-shaped shortbreads were traditionally baked at Christmas, but today shortbreads are universally eaten at any time in many varying sizes and shapes — either in their simple buttery form, or with a sprinkle of spices, nuts or other flavourings.

✳ orange, ginger & walnut
shortbread

250 g (9 oz) butter, cut into even cubes
145 g (5 1/2 oz/2/3 cup) caster (superfine) sugar
1 1/2 teaspoons natural vanilla extract
2 teaspoons finely grated orange zest
310 g (11 oz/2 1/2 cups) plain (all-purpose) flour
1 teaspoon ground ginger
60 g (2 1/4 oz/1/2 cup) walnuts, chopped

makes about 32 pieces

Beat the butter and sugar using electric beaters until pale and creamy. Mix in the vanilla and orange zest. Sift the flour and ginger together twice, then gradually stir into the creamed butter until the mixture comes together to form a soft dough. Mix in the walnuts. Gather into a ball, then flatten to a fat disc. Cover with plastic wrap and refrigerate for 30 minutes.

Meanwhile, preheat the oven to 170°C (325/Gas 3). Line two baking trays with baking paper.

Roll out the dough on a lightly floured surface until about 8 mm (3/8 inch) thick. Stamp out shapes using a 5 cm (2 inch) biscuit (cookie) cutter, then re-roll the pastry scraps and repeat. You can also use a sharp knife to cut the dough into squares or fingers — this may result in more or fewer pieces of shortbread, depending on how large or small you decide to cut them.

Place the shortbreads on the baking trays, prick each with a fork and bake for 18–20 minutes, or until pale golden.

VARIATIONS: You can vary the final flavour by adding a teaspoon of your favourite spice, such as cinnamon, cardamom, fennel or wattleseed. A change of citrus zest (e.g. lemon, lime or mandarin) or nut (e.g. macadamia, almond or pecan) will open up a whole new world of flavours, but add some finely chopped dried or glacé fruit (such as cherries, ginger, apricots or currants) and you will find yourself in connoisseur territory. If you like your shortbread sweeter, sprinkle some sugar on top before baking, or dip into melted chocolate after baking and allow to set before serving.

The macadamia is an oil-rich nut native to eastern Australia that just happens to make the most wonderfully rich, moist cakes. I remember collecting hessian bags full of macadamias from my dad's friend's property, bringing them home and spending hours trying to crack through their thick, rock-hard shells with a hammer, or by squashing them under the leg of a chair — yep, hours of fun. Fortunately, macadamias are now available already shelled, making cooking with this fantastic nut much less laborious. Lace the accompanying delectable lime syrup with a splash of rum and you'll be instantly transported to the tropics.

macadamia cake
with lime syrup

200 g (7 oz/1¼ cups) macadamia nuts
185 g (6½ oz/1½ cups) self-raising flour
½ teaspoon bicarbonate of soda (baking soda)
200 g (7 oz) unsalted butter, softened
230 g (8½ oz/1 cup) caster (superfine) sugar
4 large eggs
1 teaspoon natural vanilla extract
2 teaspoons finely grated lime zest
80 ml (2½ fl oz/⅓ cup) milk

LIME SYRUP
170 g (6 oz/¾ cup) caster (superfine) sugar
3 teaspoons finely julienned lime zest
80 ml (2½ fl oz/⅓ cup) lime juice
1 tablespoon rum, optional

serves 10–12

Preheat the oven to 160°C (315°F/Gas 2–3). Grease a 25 cm (10 inch) wide, 9 cm (3½ inch) deep, non-stick bundt tin or other scalloped-edge ring cake tin.

Very finely grind the macadamias in a food processor or in several batches in a blender, then tip into a mixing bowl. Sift the flour and bicarbonate of soda over the top and combine well.

Beat the butter and sugar using electric beaters until pale and creamy. Add the eggs, one at a time, beating well after each addition. Beat in the vanilla and lime zest. Mix in half the flour mixture, then half the milk. Repeat with the remaining flour mixture and milk, until all the ingredients are well combined. Spoon into the prepared tin and smooth over. Bake for 45 minutes, or until the cake is dark golden and comes away slightly from the side of the tin. A skewer inserted into the centre should come out clean.

Allow the cake to rest in the tin on a wire rack for 10 minutes, before inverting onto the rack to cool completely. (If you tip the cake out of the tin before this time it may collapse.)

To make the lime syrup, put the sugar, lime zest, lime juice and 125 ml (4 fl oz/½ cup) water in a small saucepan and stir over high heat until the sugar has dissolved. Boil for 5 minutes, or until slightly syrupy. Lift out the lime zest with a fork and set aside as a garnish. Take the syrup off the heat and stir in the rum, if using.

Brush the syrup evenly over the entire cake surface. Decorate the top of the cake with the reserved lime zest and serve with whipped cream or vanilla ice cream. This cake keeps well — wrap it thoroughly in plastic and store at room temperature for a few days, or refrigerate for a week (or even freeze for up to 1 month).

*with a cuppa [page 117]

chapter four * mum's DINNERS

MY MOTHER OFTEN JOKES THAT SHE STOPPED COOKING THE DAY I STARTED — WELL SHE PROBABLY DIDN'T HAVE A CHOICE! I PRETTY MUCH TOOK OVER THE KITCHEN, SPENDING HOUR UPON HOUR EXPERIMENTING AND MAKING A MESS — BUT SHE WAS ALWAYS THERE WITH A WATCHFUL EYE AND GUIDED ME THROUGH THE HARD STUFF. SHE WILL LAUGH BUT I LEARNT A LOT ABOUT FOOD FROM MUM, WHO DID ALL THE COOKING BEFORE ME. MY DAD, ALTHOUGH HE NEVER SET FOOT IN THE KITCHEN EXCEPT TO DIP A SPOON INTO SOMETHING BUBBLING ON THE STOVE OR TO RAID THE CHRISTMAS CAKE, LOVED HIS FOOD AND WAS MOST ENCOURAGING OF MY CULINARY MEDDLINGS, ALWAYS THE WILLING GUINEA PIG. BETWEEN MUM AND I, THE FAMILY WAS INDEED WELL FED.
I HAVE BEEN EXPERIMENTING AND LEARNING EVER SINCE, AND HAVING A JOB THAT INVOLVES CONSTANTLY DEVELOPING RECIPES MEANS THERE IS ALWAYS SOMETHING NEW ON THE HORIZON. BUT IT'S THE DISHES THAT MUM COOKED UP THAT I REMEMBER SO FONDLY: THE FOODS WE ALL REMEMBER FROM CHILDHOOD — COMFORT FOODS THAT NEVER SEEMED TO HAVE A RECIPE. THEY CAME FROM THE HEART AND WERE MADE WITH LOVE AND YOU COULD REALLY TASTE IT.

* roasted tomato soup with parsley cream * pumpkin soup with thai flavours * scotch broth * fish & chips with tartare sauce * crumbed veal cutlets with tomato glaze * meat pies * irish stew * creamy fish pie * macaroni cheese * creamy chicken & tarragon casserole * quiche * corned beef with caper white sauce * shepherd's pie * bangers & mash * meatloaf * roast lamb with mint sauce * roast chicken with bread sauce * roast loin of pork with apple sauce * roast beef with horseradish cream * lasagne * spaghetti bolognese * apricot chicken

❄ *The ubiquitous tin of tomato soup was a staple in every kitchen cupboard during my childhood. It's one of those memory foods which is especially warming and comforting when you're at home with the winter sniffles. When you are short on time, soup from a tin is always useful of course, but much more satisfying is this wonderfully rich tomato soup, dressed up with a herbed cream for grown-ups or served unadorned for kids — perhaps with a jumble of buttered toast soldiers or some grilled cheese on toast.*

roasted tomato soup
with parsley cream

3 kg (6 lb 12 oz) ripe roma (plum) tomatoes,
  cut into quarters
1 large red onion, chopped
2 large carrots, chopped
1 red capsicum (pepper), chopped
5 garlic cloves, peeled
80 ml (2½ fl oz/⅓ cup) olive oil
sea salt flakes, for sprinkling
500 ml (17 fl oz/2 cups) chicken stock
1½ teaspoons finely chopped thyme
1 bay leaf

PARSLEY CREAM
250 ml (9 fl oz/1 cup) pouring (whipping) cream
1 small thyme sprig
1 large handful of flat-leaf (Italian) parsley,
  very finely chopped

serves 4–6

Preheat the oven to 180°C (350°F/Gas 4). Put the tomato quarters, onion, carrot, capsicum and garlic in a roasting tin. Drizzle with the olive oil and sprinkle with sea salt flakes. Roast for 2½ hours, or until the tomato skins are quite shrivelled and the onion and carrot are golden.

Pour the stock into a large saucepan and add the thyme, bay leaf and the roasted vegetables. Bring to the boil over high heat, then reduce the heat to low and simmer for 45 minutes.

Meanwhile, begin making the parsley cream. Put the cream in a small saucepan with the thyme and bring to the boil. Reduce the heat and simmer for 25 minutes, or until thickened slightly. Sieve into a small bowl and set aside.

Remove the bay leaf and thyme sprig from the soup, then process the soup to a thick purée. Pour through a sieve into a clean saucepan, pressing on the solids to extract as much liquid as possible. Season to taste and gently reheat.

Stir the parsley into the cream mixture. Serve the soup in bowls with a swirl of the parsley cream on top. Serve any remaining cream in a separate bowl for people to swirl into their soup.

pumpkin soup
with thai flavours

Pumpkin soup is a favourite standby recipe, but is often a little lacking in flavour. This version is pumped full of aromatic Thai herbs and spices and is made creamy with coconut milk, bringing a fresh and modern twist to a recipe most of us can cook from memory. This makes a lovely change to traditional pumpkin soup and demonstrates how easy it is to borrow a few ingredients from other cuisines and turn bland into brilliant.

PUMPKIN SOUP

1 tablespoon peanut oil
1 large brown onion, chopped
10 g (1/4 oz) fresh ginger, peeled & finely chopped
3 garlic cloves, finely chopped
1 small red chilli, seeds removed & finely chopped
1 teaspoon ground cumin
1/4 teaspoon ground coriander
1/4 teaspoon ground white pepper
1 butternut pumpkin (squash), about
    1.3 kg/3 lb in total, peeled, seeded & cut into
    3 cm (1 1/4 inch) cubes
2 coriander (cilantro) roots, rinsed well &
    finely chopped
1 whole lemon grass stem, bruised well
2 makrut (kaffir lime) leaves, crushed
375 ml (13 fl oz/1 1/2 cups) chicken stock
400 ml (14 fl oz) coconut milk

coconut cream, optional, for drizzling
1 spring onion (scallion), finely sliced
2 tablespoons peanuts, toasted & finely chopped
1 handful of coriander (cilantro) leaves
lime cheeks, to serve, optional

serves 6

To make the pumpkin soup, heat the peanut oil in a large saucepan over medium–high heat, add the onion and sauté for 5 minutes, or until lightly golden. Add the ginger, garlic, chilli, cumin, ground coriander and white pepper and stir for 30 seconds, or until fragrant.

Add the remaining soup ingredients and 250 ml (9 fl oz/1 cup) water (cut the lemon grass into pieces if the stem is too large for your pot). Bring to the boil over high heat, then reduce the heat and simmer for 30 minutes, or until the pumpkin is very tender and breaking up. Remove the lemon grass and lime leaves, then purée the soup until smooth. Season to taste with salt.

Ladle the soup into bowls and drizzle with coconut cream, if desired. Garnish with the spring onion, peanuts and coriander. Serve with lime cheeks on the side for squeezing over if desired.

scotch broth

No prizes for guessing where this dish originated (hint: somewhere cold with kilts). This simple, flavoursome broth with tender chunks of lamb, vegetables and barley makes a hearty, nutritious meal. The adults-only version is enhanced with a splash of Scotch whisky — a wintery must!

1½ tablespoons olive oil
1 kg (2 lb 4 oz) lamb neck or shoulder chops, trimmed of any excess fat
1 large brown onion, chopped
1 garlic clove, crushed
1 bay leaf
1½ teaspoons finely chopped thyme
1.75 litres (61 fl oz/7 cups) chicken stock
2 large carrots
2 celery stalks
2 small turnips
1 parsnip
1 leek
125 g (4½ oz/heaped ½ cup) pearl barley, rinsed
155 g (5½ oz/1 cup) fresh or thawed frozen peas
1 handful of flat-leaf (Italian) parsley, finely chopped
1 tablespoon lemon juice
Scotch whisky, to taste, optional

serves 6

Heat 1 tablespoon of the olive oil in a very large saucepan or stockpot over medium–high heat. Lightly season the lamb chops. Working in several batches, add the chops to the oil and brown well on both sides, then remove from the pot. Add the remaining oil to the pot, if needed, and sauté the onion for 5 minutes, or until softened and lightly golden. Add the garlic and cook for 30 seconds. Put the lamb back in with the bay leaf, thyme, stock and 1.5 litres (52 fl oz/6 cups) water. Bring to the boil over high heat, then reduce the heat and simmer for 1½ hours, spooning off any impurities that rise to the surface.

Meanwhile, cut the carrots, celery, turnips and parsnip into 1.5 cm (5/8 inch) dice. Trim the leek, leaving 2 cm (3/4 inch) of green stem attached, and rinse well to remove any grit. Finely slice the leek.

Add the diced vegetables, leek and barley to the pot and simmer for another 2 hours, adding the peas in the final 10 minutes. By this stage the lamb should be falling off the bone and the vegetables and barley tender. Remove the lamb chops, pull the meat off the bones and chop. Discard the bones and any gristle. Return the meat to the pot to heat through. Stir in the parsley and lemon juice and season to taste. Add a splash of whisky to taste if desired, and serve immediately with some crusty bread.

VARIATIONS: You can use dried peas instead of fresh — just add them with the barley. You can also add some diced potato or sliced cabbage when you add the vegetables. A little pouring (whipping) cream stirred in towards the end of cooking will also enrich the broth.

I love the beach, but I prefer to visit later in the afternoon or early evening when I can dangle my legs over the edge of a rock wall and watch the waters ebb and flow without frying myself silly. Sharing a paper parcel full of piping hot, golden fish and chips with a friend is the very best way to watch the sun go down — but how often do we get to do such things these days? Never mind, whip up a batch of crispy beer-battered fish, spiced chips and creamy tartare sauce, pour yourself a glass of your favourite white wine and perch yourself on the back step for a moon viewing. Who needs the beach?

fish & chips
with tartare sauce

4 large pontiac or other all-purpose potatoes
185 g (6½ oz/1½ cups) plain (all-purpose) flour
330 ml (11¼ fl oz/1⅓ cups) beer
a pinch of cayenne pepper
¼ teaspoon sweet paprika
2 teaspoons sea salt flakes
olive oil, for deep-frying
800 g (1 lb 12 oz) flathead fillets, cut in
    half lengthways
lemon wedges, to serve

TARTARE SAUCE
160 g (5½ oz/⅔ cup) good-quality whole-egg
    mayonnaise
1½ tablespoons finely chopped white onion
2 tablespoons capers, rinsed & finely chopped
3 small, sweet, spiced gherkins (pickles),
    finely chopped
1 garlic clove, crushed
1½ teaspoons finely chopped tarragon
1 small handful of flat-leaf (Italian) parsley,
    finely chopped
3 teaspoons chardonnay vinegar or white wine
    vinegar
2 teaspoons dijon mustard

serves 4

Bring a large saucepan of water to the boil. Peel the potatoes, cut them into thick chips, then add to the saucepan. Bring to the boil and allow to cook for 5 minutes. Drain well, then spread the chips out on a clean tea towel (dish towel) to dry completely.

Put all the tartare sauce ingredients in a small bowl. Mix together thoroughly and refrigerate until ready to serve.

Combine the flour and beer with 2 teaspoons salt in a wide, shallow bowl and set aside.

Put the cayenne pepper, paprika and sea salt flakes in a small bowl and crush together using the back of a spoon. Set aside.

Fill a deep-fryer or large heavy-based saucepan one-third full of olive oil and heat to 180°C (350°F), or until a cube of bread dropped into the oil browns in 15 seconds. Cook the potato chips in two batches for 10–12 minutes per batch, or until lightly golden, then drain well on paper towels and set aside.

Dip the fish in the beer batter and deep-fry in several batches for 5 minutes at a time, or until the batter is golden and the fish is just cooked through. Drain on paper towels and keep warm in a low oven.

Meanwhile, deep-fry the chips for a second time for 2 minutes, or until lovely and crisp. Drain on paper towels, then toss with the salt and spice mixture. Serve the fish and chips with the tartare sauce and lemon wedges on the side. The perfect accompaniment is a crisp, cool wedge of iceberg lettuce.

crumbed veal cutlets
with tomato glaze

2 tablespoons plain (all-purpose) flour
4 veal cutlets, each 3–4 cm (1¼–1½ inches) thick
1 egg, lightly beaten
2 garlic cloves, crushed
1 teaspoon very finely chopped thyme or sage
100 g (3½ oz/1 cup) ground almonds
100 g (3½ oz/1 cup) grated parmesan cheese
olive oil, for pan-frying
lemon wedges, to serve, optional

TOMATO GLAZE
3 teaspoons tomato paste (concentrated purée)
330 ml (11¼ fl oz/1⅓ cups) rich beef stock
½ teaspoon caster (superfine) sugar
1 garlic clove, bruised
1 thyme or sage sprig

serves 4

Season the flour with salt and ground black pepper and use it to lightly coat the veal. Combine the egg, garlic and thyme or sage in a wide, shallow bowl. Combine the ground almonds and parmesan on a small plate. Dip the cutlets into the egg and allow any excess to drip off, then firmly press both sides of each cutlet into the almond mixture. Cover and refrigerate for an hour or two to set the crumb mixture.

Meanwhile, put all the tomato glaze ingredients in a small saucepan over high heat, stir well and bring to the boil. Reduce to a simmer and cook for 10 minutes, or until thickened and glazy. Keep warm, or reheat gently while the cutlets are cooking and strain into a jug before serving.

Place a frying pan over medium heat and pour in enough olive oil to come 5 mm (¼ inch) up the side of the pan. When the oil is hot, cook the cutlets for 5 minutes on each side, or until the crumbs are golden. The meat should still be a little pink inside. Drain on paper towels and allow to rest for a few minutes, then serve with the tomato glaze and some lemon wedges for squeezing over, if desired.

VARIATION: Veal cutlets not your thing? Use the same method for pork or lamb cutlets, or to make chicken, pork or veal schnitzel.

Crumbed cutlets never tasted this good when I was growing up (sorry mum)! The meat is tender, with a hint of garlic and thyme, and the coating is a crunchy, golden cloak made from ground almonds and grated parmesan cheese. Okay, so I stole the idea from the Italians and their 'costolette parmigiana' — after all, a recipe that's over 400 years old has to be all right.

✳ *In the early days of the humble meat pie, the pastry case merely served as a cooking and serving vessel and was often barely edible — thank heavens someone scrapped that crazy idea. Here, flaky, golden pastry encases a hearty filling of tender, chunky beef in a rich sauce flavoured with beer and... wait for it, Vegemite! Serve with creamy mashed potato (see page 145) or a salad.*

meat pies

2 tablespoons olive oil

1 brown onion, finely chopped

2 tablespoons plain (all-purpose) flour

600 g (1 lb 5 oz) chuck steak, cut into
1.5 cm (5/8 inch) dice

10 g (1/4 oz) butter

250 ml (9 fl oz/1 cup) beer

375 ml (13 fl oz/1 1/2 cups) beef stock

1 small carrot, finely diced

1 celery stalk, finely diced

2 garlic cloves, crushed

2 teaspoons Vegemite, or other yeast extract such as
Marmite or Promite

1 1/2 tablespoons tomato paste (concentrated purée)

1 tablespoon worcestershire sauce

1 bay leaf

3 sheets of ready-made shortcrust (pie) pastry

3 sheets of ready-made puff pastry

1 egg, lightly beaten

makes 6 individual pies

Heat 1 tablespoon of the oil in a heavy-based saucepan over medium–high heat. Add the onion and sauté for 10 minutes, or until golden. Remove from the pan and set aside.

Season the flour with salt and black pepper and use it to lightly coat the beef cubes all over. Add the remaining oil and the butter to the pan. Sauté the beef in three batches until lightly browned all over, adding more oil if needed. Set aside.

Add the beer and stock to the pan, scraping up any cooked-on bits. Return the beef and onion to the pan with the carrot, celery, garlic, Vegemite, tomato paste, worcestershire sauce and bay leaf. Bring to the boil, then reduce the heat and simmer for 1 1/4 hours, or until the beef is very tender and the sauce is thick and rich. Discard the bay leaf and season to taste. Allow to cool slightly, then cover and refrigerate for 4 hours, or until cold.

Put two baking trays in the oven and preheat the oven to 200°C (400°F/Gas 6). Cut six 14.5 cm (5 3/4 inch) diameter circles from the shortcrust pastry and six 12.5 cm (4 3/4 inch) circles from the puff pastry. Line the bases of six pie tins measuring 12.5 cm (4 3/4 inches) across the top, 7.5 cm (3 inches) across the base and 3.5 cm (1 1/3 inches) deep with the shortcrust pastry circles — the pastry should come just a little way above the edge of the tins. Brush the edges lightly with the beaten egg. Divide the chilled beef mixture between the lined pie tins. Lay a puff pastry circle over the top of each pie and press down around the edges of the shortcrust pastry, pinching together if you like to help the edges adhere.

Pierce a little air vent in the top of each pie using the tip of a small, sharp knife. Brush the top of the pies with the egg, avoiding the vent, and place directly onto the trays in the hot oven. Bake for 10 minutes, or until the pastry is puffed and lightly golden, then lower the oven temperature to 180°C (350°F/Gas 4) and cook for a further 15 minutes, or until the pastry is golden and the filling hot.

VARIATION: Make little pot pies by filling individual ramekins with the beef and topping with a puff pastry lid. Cook for 10 minutes at 200°C (400°F/Gas 6), then 8 minutes at 180°C (350°F/Gas 4).

Based on two iconically Irish ingredients, lamb and potatoes, this wholesome stew, originally a cold-weather peasant dish cooked over an open fire, proves how just a few simple ingredients can produce a wonderfully flavoursome and comforting meal in a bowl. I have used shanks, a popular cut these days, but you can also use chops or diced lamb.

irish stew

6 lamb shanks, about 1.6 kg (3 lb 8 oz) in total

1 tablespoon olive oil

330 ml (11¼ fl oz/1⅓ cups) Guinness or other dark beer

2 teaspoons soft brown sugar

1 litre (35 fl oz/4 cups) lamb or chicken stock

2 leeks, white part only, sliced

12 baby potatoes

1 large floury potato, cut into 1 cm (½ inch) dice

2 teaspoons finely chopped thyme

3 teaspoons plain (all-purpose) flour

15 g (½ oz) butter, softened

1 handful of flat-leaf (Italian) parsley or mint, shredded

serves 4–6

Season the lamb shanks with salt and freshly cracked black pepper. Heat the olive oil in a large stockpot or very large saucepan over medium–high heat, then brown the lamb shanks well in two batches — this should take about 5 minutes per batch. Set aside. Tip any residual fat out of the pot, then add the Guinness, sugar, stock and 500 ml (17 fl oz/2 cups) water, scraping up any cooked-on bits as the mixture comes to the boil.

Put the shanks back in the pot, along with the leek, baby potatoes, diced potato and thyme. Bring to the boil again, skimming off any oil and foam that rises to the surface. Reduce to a simmer, then cover and cook for 2 hours, or until the shanks are very tender.

Remove the shanks and baby potatoes using tongs and a slotted spoon. Cover and set aside. Bring the sauce to the boil, then cook for 15 minutes or until thickened slightly, crushing up any potato cubes that have not disintegrated.

Mix the flour and butter to a smooth paste, then whisk a teaspoon at a time into the sauce. Simmer for a couple of minutes, or until the sauce has thickened to a coating consistency. Return the meat and vegetables to the pot and stir to combine and warm through. Stir in the parsley or mint and season to taste.

Although my dad and his brothers loved to fish and often brought home a decent catch, fish dinners were not a huge hit in our house. Particularly fish pie, which dad's sister cooked for us one Friday lunch, filled with tuna in a Vegemite sauce! But when I wrote this recipe I wondered why I'd waited so long to discover a good fish pie, and why more people don't cook it today. It's a great way to serve fish in winter when you crave something substantial from the seafood world.

creamy fish pie

60 g (2¼ oz) butter

2 leeks, white part only, sliced

1 large fennel bulb (about 500 g/1 lb 2 oz), finely sliced (reserve the fennel tips for the sauce)

1 celery stalk, finely diced

1 large garlic clove, crushed

1 kg (2 lb 4 oz) boneless, skinless white fish fillets, such as snapper, flathead, blue-eye or ling

80 ml (2½ fl oz/⅓ cup) dry white wine or vermouth

2 bay leaves

1 teaspoon white peppercorns

a few parsley stalks

a few celery leaves

40 g (1½ oz/⅓ cup) plain (all-purpose) flour

a large pinch of freshly grated nutmeg

250 ml (9 fl oz/1 cup) milk

250 g (9 oz/1 cup) crème fraîche or sour cream

2 teaspoons dijon mustard

1 tablespoon lemon juice

1½ tablespoons finely chopped fennel tips or dill

TOPPING

16 slices of white bread, crusts removed

softened butter, for spreading

1 handful of flat-leaf (Italian) parsley, finely chopped

75 g (2½ oz/¾ cup) finely grated parmesan cheese

serves 6–8

Melt a third of the butter in a saucepan over medium heat and add the leek and fennel. Cook, stirring occasionally, for 10 minutes, or until soft. Add the celery and garlic and sauté for 5 minutes, or until the celery is tender. Remove from the pan and set aside, but keep the pan at the ready for continuing the sauce.

Put the fish, wine, bay leaves, peppercorns, parsley stalks, celery leaves and 1 teaspoon salt in a large saucepan, then add enough cold water to cover. Slowly bring to the boil over medium heat, removing the fish with a slotted spoon as soon as it becomes opaque. Continue to cook the stock for a further 15 minutes, then strain and keep warm over low heat. When the fish is cool enough to handle, break it into large flakes.

Add the remaining butter to the same pan you sautéed the fennel in and place over medium–high heat. When the butter begins to sizzle, stir in the flour and nutmeg and cook for 1 minute. Gradually whisk in 750 ml (26 fl oz/3 cups) of the warm fish stock until smooth. Whisk in the milk and continue whisking for 5 minutes, or until very smooth and thickened slightly. Stir in the reserved fennel mixture and cook for a further 5 minutes, stirring occasionally.

Take the pan off the heat, then stir in the crème fraîche, mustard, lemon juice and fennel tips or dill. Season well. Carefully fold the sauce through the fish, trying not to break it up too much, then pour into a large, well-greased ceramic baking dish. Cover and refrigerate for 2 hours, or until ready to cook.

Preheat the oven to 190°C (375°F/Gas 5). To make the topping, spread the bread with softened butter, cut into small cubes and toss with the parsley and parmesan. Scatter evenly over the top of the fish mixture. Bake for 40–45 minutes, or until the topping is crunchy and golden and the filling is hot.

VARIATIONS: Replace the fish or half the fish with some cooked prawns (shrimp) and scallops and add a tablespoon of finely chopped capers. You can also use good-quality tinned or bottled tuna and a ready-made fish stock to save time.

✳ macaroni cheese

500 g (1 lb 2 oz) macaroni or penne
60 g (2¼ oz) butter
1 teaspoon very finely chopped sage
¼ teaspoon very finely chopped rosemary
1 brown onion, chopped
3 tablespoons plain (all-purpose) flour
685 ml (23½ fl oz/2¾ cups) milk
375 ml (13 fl oz/1½ cups) pouring (whipping) cream
1 garlic clove, crushed
2 teaspoons dijon mustard or wholegrain mustard
350 g (12 oz/2¾ cups) grated sharp cheddar cheese, or
   a mixture of cheddar & various cheeses including
   parmesan, fontina, gruyère & blue
1 small handful of flat-leaf (Italian) parsley
½ bunch chives, snipped
80 g (2¾ oz/1 cup) fresh white breadcrumbs

serves 4–6

Bring a large saucepan of salted water to the boil. Add the pasta and cook according to the packet instructions, or until *al dente*. Drain well.

Preheat the grill (broiler) to medium–high.

Melt a third of the butter in a saucepan over medium–high heat and add the sage, rosemary and onion. Sauté for 5 minutes, or until the onion has softened, then remove from the pan. Melt the remaining butter in the pan, then add the flour and cook for 1 minute. Remove from the heat and gradually whisk in the milk and cream until smooth. Place back over the heat and stir constantly until the mixture boils and thickens.

Remove from the heat and stir in the garlic, mustard and two-thirds of the cheese until smooth. Combine the cheese mixture with the pasta and half the parsley and chives. Season to taste. Pour into a greased 2 litre (70 fl oz/8-cup capacity) heatproof dish and smooth over the top.

Combine the breadcrumbs with the remaining cheese and herbs, and evenly sprinkle over the pasta. Cook under the hot grill for a few minutes, or until the cheese is golden and bubbling. Serve.

VARIATIONS: Add green vegetables such as peas or broccoli for extra nutrition. Or spoon some chunky tomato or bolognese sauce (see page 159) into the baking dish before topping with the macaroni cheese for a layered effect. Perhaps add some bacon, ham, chicken or tuna or sautéed mushrooms for flavour — or some chopped celery, walnuts and apple for extra texture and to help cut through the richness. Change the herbs to your favourites or add a little spice such as cumin, chilli or paprika — it's so easy to put your own stamp on this simple dish.

Although the macaroni and cheese that most of us know today is commonly believed to be an American creation (being widely available as a boxed commercial product since 1937), its ownership is also claimed by the English, who it is said brought back macaroni — and the idea of combining it with cheese — from Italy in the 1700s, after which they promptly threw a bit of cream into the mix and baked it! Whatever its origins, we all have our own adaptations. This is pure soothe food and great for rainy days curled up with a good book — a winner with kids and adults alike.

Every mum has her own special rendition of chicken casserole. This is a tweaked version of my mum's French-inspired recipe, which happens to be the dish I requested every year for my birthday dinner for about 10 years running! It was an addiction I did manage to beat — but I do still love it occasionally.

creamy chicken & tarragon casserole

1 tablespoon olive oil

10 g (1/4 oz) butter

6 boneless, skinless chicken breasts (about 250 g/
   9 oz each), with wing bone attached

2 slices of bacon, cut into 2 cm (3/4 inch) pieces

2 celery stalks, finely diced

6 thick spring onions (scallions), cut into 4 cm
   (1 1/2 inch) lengths

2 garlic cloves, crushed

2 teaspoons plain (all-purpose) flour

125 ml (4 fl oz/1/2 cup) chardonnay or riesling

375 ml (13 fl oz/1 1/2 cups) chicken stock

310 ml (10 3/4 oz/1 1/4 cups) pouring (whipping) cream

1 tablespoon dijon mustard

1 tablespoon lemon juice

3 teaspoons finely chopped tarragon, plus extra,
   to garnish

serves 6

Preheat the oven to 180°C (350°F/Gas 4). Heat the oil and butter in a flameproof casserole dish over medium–high heat. Season the chicken with salt and a little freshly cracked black pepper. Working in three batches, brown the chicken well all over — this should take about 4 minutes per batch. Set aside. Add the bacon, celery and spring onions to the casserole dish and cook, stirring occasionally, for 5 minutes, or until the bacon and onions are lightly golden. Set aside with the chicken.

Add the garlic to the casserole dish and cook for 30 seconds, or until fragrant, then stir in the flour and cook for 30 seconds. Gradually stir in the wine, stock, cream, mustard, lemon juice and tarragon until well combined, scraping up any cooked-on bits. Return the chicken and resting juices, bacon and vegetables to the casserole and stir to combine. Tuck the chicken breasts down so they are covered by the other ingredients.

Bake for 35–40 minutes, or until the chicken is just cooked through and tender. Remove the chicken with a slotted spoon, cover and set aside. Put the casserole dish back over high heat and bring to the boil. Cook for 10–12 minutes, or until the sauce has thickened to a coating consistency. Season to taste, put the chicken back in and gently reheat.

Serve garnished with a little extra chopped tarragon, accompanied by mashed potato or rice, and perhaps a crisp green salad or some lightly cooked asparagus or sugar snap peas.

For all those 'real men' who claim they don't eat quiche, let's call this a fancy bacon and egg pie instead — sound better? This French classic (with Germanic roots) makes a splendidly light, simple dinner when served with a crisp green salad. And it's not too shabby as a special-occasion breakfast dish either.

quiche

PASTRY

185 g (6^{1}/$_2$ oz/1^{1}/$_2$ cups) plain (all-purpose) flour

125 g (4^{1}/$_2$ oz) cold butter, diced

1 tablespoon iced water

FILLING

20 g (^{3}/$_4$ oz) butter

1 brown onion, chopped

^{1}/$_2$ teaspoon very finely chopped thyme

2 slices of bacon, cut into thin strips

130 g (4^{3}/$_4$ oz/1 cup) grated gruyère or cheddar cheese

5 large eggs

310 ml (10^{3}/$_4$ fl oz/1^{1}/$_4$ cups) pouring (whipping) cream

1 small handful of flat-leaf (Italian) parsley,
  finely chopped

a large pinch of nutmeg

serves 6

To make the pastry, sift the flour into a bowl and rub in the butter with your fingertips until the mixture resembles fine breadcrumbs. Gradually add the iced water while cutting into the mixture with a flat-bladed knife, until it just comes together to form a soft dough. Turn out onto a lightly floured surface and gather into a ball. Wrap in plastic wrap and refrigerate for 30 minutes.

Lightly grease a deep, 22 cm (8^{1}/$_2$ inch), loose-based fluted flan (tart) tin. Roll the dough out between two sheets of baking paper until 2–3 mm (^{1}/$_{16}$–^{1}/$_8$ inch) thick and about 30 cm (12 inches) in diameter. Remove the top sheet of baking paper and invert the pastry into the prepared tin. Carefully press the pastry into the bottom of the tin. Trim off any overhanging edges with a sharp knife or by running a rolling pin over the top of the tin. Refrigerate for 30 minutes.

Preheat the oven to 190°C (375°F/Gas 5). Line the pastry with a sheet of slightly crumpled baking paper and pour in a cup of rice or beans (or use baking beads) to weigh it down. Bake for 20 minutes, then remove the paper and weights and cook for a further 15 minutes, or until the pastry is dry all over and pale golden. Remove from the oven and lower the oven temperature to 170°C (325°F/Gas 3). Place a baking tray in the oven to heat.

While the pastry is blind-baking, make the filling. Melt the butter in a saucepan over medium heat and sauté the onion, thyme and bacon for 7 minutes, or until the onion has softened and is very lightly golden. Remove from the pan and when cool, scatter the onion and bacon over the pastry base and top with the cheese. Whisk together the eggs, cream, parsley and nutmeg, lightly season, then gently pour into the pastry shell.

Put the quiche on the heated baking tray and bake for 30 minutes, or until the egg has just set. The filling will still be very slightly wobbly. Remove from the oven and allow to rest for 10 minutes before serving.

VARIATIONS: Quiches lend themselves to all manner of flavours so feel free to add other vegetables, meats, seafood, herbs and cheeses. Also, it's fine to speed things up by using a ready-made pastry if you are short on time.

✳ *Before refrigeration, meat had to be preserved by other means, one of them being corning — a method of curing with coarse salt. Beef is still corned today but in a brine solution, and is done so more as a variation in flavour and texture than a preservation method. Corned beef is commonly served with cabbage, so feel free to pop a few wedges into the pot with the other vegetables if you are a traditionalist. A creamy white sauce is the perfect accompaniment.*

corned beef
with caper white sauce

1.5 kg (3 lb 5 oz) corned beef silverside
1 brown onion, cut in half
8 cloves
1 teaspoon peppercorns
1½ teaspoons allspice berries
2 bay leaves
6 garlic cloves
90 g (3¼ oz/¼ cup) golden syrup or soft brown sugar
125 ml (4 fl oz/½ cup) cider vinegar
12 bulb spring onions (scallions), trimmed leaving
   2 cm (¾ inch) of stem attached, optional
12 baby carrots, trimmed
24 baby beans, topped & tailed
30 g (1 oz) butter
1 large handful of flat-leaf (Italian) parsley, or
   1 small handful of chervil, finely chopped

CAPER WHITE SAUCE
30 g (1 oz) butter
2 tablespoons plain (all-purpose) flour
185 ml (6 fl oz/¾ cup) reserved corned beef
   cooking liquid, kept warm
310 ml (10¾ fl oz/1¼ cups) milk
1 tablespoon capers, rinsed & finely chopped
1 teaspoon dijon mustard

serves 4–6

Rinse the beef, then place in a large saucepan. Spear each onion half with four cloves, then add to the pot with the peppercorns, allspice, bay leaves, garlic cloves, golden syrup and vinegar. Pour in enough cold water to cover the meat well. Slowly bring to the boil, spooning off any impurities that rise to the surface, then reduce to a simmer. Cover and cook for 2–2¼ hours, or until the meat is very tender when tested with a skewer through the thickest part. Top up with extra water if needed during cooking.

Transfer the beef to a bowl, ladle over a little of the cooking liquid to help keep it moist, then cover to keep warm. Strain the remaining liquid and set aside 185 ml (6 fl oz/¾ cup) for the caper white sauce. Return the rest of the cooking liquid to the pot and bring to the boil. Add the bulb spring onions, if using, and carrots and cook for 10 minutes, then add the beans and cook for a further 4 minutes, or until all the vegetables are just tender. Drain and toss with the butter and parsley or chervil. Season to taste.

Meanwhile, to make the caper white sauce, heat the butter in a saucepan over medium–high heat. Add the flour and cook for 1 minute. Gradually whisk in the warm reserved cooking liquid until smooth. Whisk in the milk, bring to the boil and cook for 5 minutes, stirring regularly until thickened. Remove from the heat, stir in the capers and mustard and season to taste.

Carve the meat into thick slices and serve topped with a pile of buttered vegetables and the sauce on the side for pouring over. Great with mashed or crispy roast potatoes.

VARIATION: You can add other vegetables to the cooking liquid if you like, such as baby potatoes, cabbage and broccoli, but remember that some vegetables take longer to cook than others — keep an eye on them to make sure they are tender and not mushy.

✳ shepherd's pie

2 tablespoons olive oil

1 large brown onion, chopped

2 carrots, finely diced

1 large celery stalk, finely diced

1 kg (2 lb 4 oz) minced (ground) lamb

2 garlic cloves, crushed

80 ml (2 1/2 fl oz/1/3 cup) dry white wine

1 1/2 teaspoons very finely chopped rosemary

2 tablespoons tomato paste (concentrated purée)

500 ml (17 fl oz/2 cups) lamb stock, or 250 ml
   (9 fl oz/1 cup) each chicken & beef stock

2 tablespoons worcestershire sauce

1 bay leaf

a large pinch of finely ground fresh nutmeg

100 g (3 1/2 oz/2/3 cup) thawed frozen peas

1 kg (2 lb 4 oz) desiree or other mashing potatoes,
   peeled & cut into large chunks

80 g (2 3/4 oz) butter, melted

185 ml (6 fl oz/3/4 cup) pouring (whipping) cream

1 handful of flat-leaf (Italian) parsley, chopped

85 g (3 oz/2/3 cup) grated sharp cheddar cheese,
   optional

serves 6

Heat 1 tablespoon of the olive oil in a large, deep-sided frying pan over medium–high heat. Add the onion, carrot and celery and sauté for 15 minutes, or until lightly golden, then remove from the heat. Increase the heat to high and add the remaining oil to the pan. Brown the lamb mince well in three batches, for about 3 minutes per batch, breaking up any lumps with the back of a spoon. Remove from the pan and add to the vegetables.

Add the garlic, wine, rosemary and tomato paste to the pan, stir well and cook for 30 seconds. Add the mince and vegetables, along with the stock, worcestershire sauce, bay leaf and nutmeg. Bring to the boil, then reduce the heat and simmer for 45 minutes.

Take the pan off the heat and stir in the peas. Season to taste and allow to cool slightly before transferring to a wide, shallow, non-metallic 4 litre (140 fl oz/16-cup capacity) baking dish. Refrigerate until completely cold — this helps the base to firm up slightly so the mashed potato won't sink into it too easily when you spoon it over the top.

Preheat the oven to 200°C (400°F/Gas 6). Put the potatoes in a large saucepan, cover with water and bring to the boil. Cook for 12–15 minutes, or until very tender, then drain well. Add the butter and most of the cream and mash together until very smooth, adding the remaining cream if necessary. Stir in the parsley and cheese, if using, and season to taste. Carefully dollop the potato over the chilled lamb mixture and smooth it over or make swirls or decorative patterns on the surface with a fork. Bake for 40–45 minutes, or until the surface is golden. Serve hot.

VARIATION: Try stirring some sliced cabbage or leek through the mashed potato. To make a cottage pie, substitute beef for the lamb and use only beef stock.

Although the English, Irish and Scottish might clash over ownership of the original shepherd's pie recipe, they unanimously agree that it consists of minced lamb and vegetables with a mashed potato topping. Variations on the theme are in circulation of course — including a well-known version made with beef instead of lamb, known as cottage pie. People often get confused as to which is which, but it's easy to remember: just ask yourself, what animals did shepherds herd?

In my line of work I get to eat a wondrous array of foods, but every so often I crave some old-fashioned pork sausages or bangers and mash. And while a splash of good tomato sauce always goes down well, I prefer a rich, savoury onion gravy — perhaps a legacy of days spent with my dad at the racetrack! While dad had his eye on the ponies, the rest of us were often found in the dining room. I knew I'd 'backed a winner' when the home-made onion gravy made an appearance — and the curried sausages too, but that's another story ...

bangers & mash

ONION & SAGE GRAVY

2 teaspoons olive oil
20 g (³/₄ oz) butter
2 teaspoons finely chopped sage
2 large brown onions, sliced
1¹/₂ tablespoons plain (all-purpose) flour
2 tablespoons beer
375 ml (13 fl oz/1¹/₂ cups) beef stock
1 teaspoon tomato paste (concentrated purée)

MASH

1 kg (2 lb 4 oz) desiree or other mashing potatoes,
    peeled & chopped
100 g (3¹/₂ oz) butter, diced
185 g (6¹/₂ oz/³/₄ cup) sour cream

8 good-quality, thick pork sausages
8 slices of bacon, streaky part only

serves 4

To make the onion and sage gravy, heat the olive oil and half the butter in a small saucepan over medium–high heat. Add most of the sage and cook for 1 minute, then add the onion and cook, stirring regularly, for 20 minutes, or until the onion is softened and golden. Remove the onion from the pan and set aside.

Add the remaining butter to the pan, then stir in the flour and cook for 1 minute. Gradually whisk in the beer and stock, then whisk in the tomato paste and allow to come to the boil. Return the onion to the pan and mix well. Bring to the boil, then reduce the heat and simmer, stirring regularly, for 10 minutes, or until the gravy is thick, rich and flavoursome. Stir in the remaining sage and season well. Cover and set aside until ready to serve.

To make the mash, put the potatoes in a large saucepan, cover with water and bring to the boil. Cook for 12–15 minutes, or until very tender, then drain well. Add the butter and sour cream and mash until very smooth. Season to taste with salt and pepper. Keep warm.

Meanwhile, wrap a slice of bacon around each sausage and secure with a toothpick. Fry the sausages in a large, lightly greased frying pan over medium–high heat for 18 minutes, or until cooked through, turning regularly. The actual timing may vary depending on the thickness of the sausages. Remove the toothpicks before serving.

While the sausages are cooking, reheat the onion gravy. Spoon the mash onto four plates, sit two sausages on top and spoon over a little sage and onion gravy. Serve hot.

It may have been an overnight sensation in the 50s but sadly, most of my childhood experiences with the savoury loaf (other than my mum's of course) were not good — often dry, tasteless and quite unpalatable. Until quite recently, mince was considered a cheap way to make a meal stretch and usually employed a low-quality cut or scraps. Fortunately that is not the case today, with many types from lean to fatty all readily available. Personally I like my mince to have decent marbelling for dishes such as meatloaf, which helps to keep it tender and moist. Seasoning is important, as are breadcrumbs to soften the mixture. A rich, gutsy sauce or gravy on the side ensures the end result is anything but humdrum.

meatloaf

8 slices of bacon, streaky part only, each 14 cm (5½ inches) long
500 g (1 lb 2 oz) minced (ground) veal or beef
500 g (1 lb 2 oz) minced (ground) pork
1 tablespoon very finely chopped sage
3 teaspoons very finely chopped thyme
1 small handful of flat-leaf (Italian) parsley, finely chopped
1 celery stalk, very finely diced
1 carrot, very finely diced
3 garlic cloves
1 large brown onion, finely chopped
2 large eggs
1 egg yolk
240 g (8½ oz/3 cups) fresh white breadcrumbs

SAUCE

60 ml (2 fl oz/¼ cup) tomato sauce (ketchup)
1 tablespoon tomato paste (concentrated purée)
1½ tablespoons worcestershire sauce
375 ml (13 fl oz/1½ cups) rich beef stock
1½ tablespoons soft brown sugar
a pinch of ground allspice

serves 6

Preheat the oven to 170°C (325°F/Gas 3). Grease a non-stick terrine or loaf (bar) tin measuring 22 x 9 cm (8½ x 3½ inches) and 9 cm (3½ inches) deep. Lay the bacon slices across the base, overlapping them slightly.

Put all the remaining meatloaf ingredients in a large bowl and, using very clean hands, mix thoroughly to combine. Season well with salt and freshly cracked black pepper. (If you have time, you can do this step the night before, which is great for allowing the flavours to develop.)

Pack the mixture into the prepared tin, but be careful not to disturb the bacon slices. Smooth over the top. Cover tightly with foil and bake for 40 minutes, then remove the foil and bake for a further 40 minutes, or until the loaf is firm to the touch and just starting to come away from the edge of the tin. Remove from the oven, cover loosely and allow to rest for at least 10 minutes, before inverting onto a serving dish.

Meanwhile, combine all the sauce ingredients in a small saucepan and stir until smooth. Place over medium–high heat until the mixture comes to the boil, then cook for 15–20 minutes, or until thick and slightly glazy. Pour into a small jug and serve at the table with the meatloaf. Great with mashed potato and lightly cooked green vegetables.

NOTE: This meatloaf is not highly seasoned as it is served with a rich sauce — if you prefer, use just half the sauce ingredients to season the mince before cooking.

✳ *Serving up a lamb roast has been a ritual around family dinner tables for as long as I can remember, yet so many people are reluctant to attempt to cook one. Seriously, it really is so simple that there's no excuse for the humble lamb roast not to be a headliner in every basic recipe repertoire — with or without the mint sauce.*

roast lamb
with mint sauce

1.8 kg (4 lb) leg of lamb
a few rosemary sprigs
4 garlic cloves, cut into slivers
olive oil, for drizzling
1½ tablespoons plain (all-purpose) flour
375 ml (13 fl oz/1½ cups) hot chicken stock

MINT SAUCE
1 large handful of fresh mint, very finely chopped
1 small spring onion (scallion), white part only,
    very finely chopped
2 tablespoons chardonnay vinegar or white
    wine vinegar
2 teaspoons caster (superfine) sugar
2 tablespoons boiling water

serves 4–6

Preheat the oven to 200°C (400°F/Gas 6). Using the tip of a small, sharp knife, make incisions all over the lamb. Break the rosemary into very small sprigs and push a little into each incision, along with a sliver of garlic. Drizzle with a little olive oil and rub the oil all over the surface. Season with salt and pepper and place on a rack in a roasting tin. Pour 125 ml (4 fl oz/½ cup) water into the base of the tin.

Roast the lamb for 15 minutes, then lower the oven temperature to 180°C (350°F/Gas 4) and cook for a further 50 minutes for a medium–rare result. Roast for an additional 10 minutes if you prefer your meat a little more well done.

While the lamb is roasting, make the mint sauce. Combine all the ingredients in a small bowl with ¼ teaspoon salt and set aside for at least 30 minutes before serving.

When the lamb is cooked, transfer to a serving dish and loosely cover with foil to keep it warm while it rests for 15 minutes. Don't skip the resting process as the meat needs to relax after being in the heat, allowing the juices to sink back through the meat, ensuring it is evenly juicy and tender. If you try to carve the meat before it has rested, the juices will run out and the meat will be dry.

While the lamb is resting, make the gravy. Place the roasting tin over one or two burners or stove hotplates over medium–high heat. Sprinkle the flour evenly over the surface and mix in with a wooden spoon. Using a balloon whisk, gradually whisk in the hot stock until the gravy is smooth, scraping up any cooked-on bits. (A balloon whisk is more effective than a wooden spoon for eliminating lumps.) Whisking occasionally, cook the gravy for a few minutes, or until thickened to a light coating consistency. Whisk in any resting juices from the lamb and season to taste.

Carve the lamb and serve with the gravy and mint sauce on the side for everyone to help themselves.

When I roast a chicken I like to roast a big one so there are leftovers the next day for a salad or scrumptious chicken sandwiches — unfortunately rarely is there anything left but the parson's nose! The simple bread sauce is a traditional British accompaniment and is particularly delicious in the cooler months.

roast chicken
with bread sauce

2 tablespoons olive oil

2 kg (4 lb 8 oz) whole chicken

2 teaspoons sea salt flakes

1 teaspoon finely chopped fresh thyme, plus
   1 large sprig

1/2 lemon

4 garlic cloves, bruised

10 g (1/4 oz) butter

1 1/2 tablespoons plain (all-purpose) flour

375 ml (13 fl oz/1 1/2 cups) hot chicken stock

BREAD SAUCE

250 ml (9 fl oz/1 cup) milk

1 bay leaf

1/2 small brown onion, roughly chopped

1 small thyme sprig

a large pinch of nutmeg

a small pinch of allspice

60 g (2 1/4 oz/3/4 cup) fresh white breadcrumbs

1 teaspoon butter

1 tablespoon pouring (whipping) cream

serves 4

Preheat the oven to 220°C (425°F/Gas 7). Rub the olive oil all over the chicken and place on a rack in a roasting tin. Sprinkle with the sea salt flakes and chopped thyme and rub all over the skin. Squeeze the juice from the lemon half over the top, then place the lemon half inside the chicken with the garlic cloves and thyme sprig. Tie the legs together with kitchen string so they hold their shape. Pour 250 ml (9 fl oz/1 cup) water into the base of the tin.

Bake the chicken for 20 minutes. Lower the oven temperature to 190°C (375°F/Gas 5) and roast for a further 45 minutes, or until the skin is evenly golden and the juices run clear when the thickest part of the thigh is pierced with the tip of a small, sharp knife.

Meanwhile, make the bread sauce. Put the milk, bay leaf, onion, thyme, nutmeg and allspice in a saucepan. Allow to just come to the boil over high heat, then reduce the heat and simmer for 5 minutes. Strain the milk, then return to the saucepan with the breadcrumbs and butter and stir for 2 minutes, or until thick and smooth. Stir in the cream and season to taste. Gently reheat just prior to serving.

When the chicken is cooked, remove to a serving dish, cover lightly with foil and allow to rest for 10 minutes. Meanwhile, make the gravy. Place the roasting tin over one or two burners or stove hotplates over medium–high heat. Add the butter and allow to melt. Sprinkle the flour evenly over the surface and mix in with a wooden spoon. Cook for 1 minute. Using a balloon whisk, gradually whisk in the hot stock until smooth, scraping up any cooked-on bits. Whisking occasionally, cook the gravy for a few minutes, or until thickened to a light coating consistency. Season to taste.

Carve the chicken and serve with the gravy and bread sauce on the side for everyone to help themselves.

VARIATION: Try using herbs such as sage, rosemary or tarragon, or sprinkle with a mix of smoked paprika, oregano and cumin. Organic chickens are wonderfully flavoursome, but note that the flesh and juices may often look a bit pink even when fully cooked.

✳ *Roast pork with crispy crackling is one of my favourite winter treats — and for me, there has to be gravy and apple sauce to complete the experience. When you buy a rolled pork loin it will have had the bone removed and the skin scored so you can cut through both the crackling and the meat easily, allowing for fuss-free serving. There is no real trick to crispy crackling — you just need salt and to have the temperature hot enough for a sufficient length of time.*

roast loin of pork with apple sauce

1 tablespoon sea salt flakes
2 kg (4 lb 8 oz) rolled pork loin (ask your butcher
   to score it for you if it's not already done)
2 tablespoons plain (all-purpose) flour
375 ml (13 fl oz/1½ cups) hot chicken stock

APPLE SAUCE
2 granny smith apples, peeled, cored & chopped
2 teaspoons lemon juice
1 tablespoon caster (superfine) sugar
¼ teaspoon ground cinnamon

serves 6

Preheat the oven to 200°C (400°F/Gas 6). Rub the sea salt flakes all over the skin of the pork and into the scoring. Tie the loin together with kitchen string. Sit the pork on a rack in a roasting tin. Roast for 1 hour 40 minutes, or until the crackling is crisp and golden — the crackling will become crisper once you take it out of the oven.

While the pork is roasting, make the apple sauce. Put the apple, lemon juice, sugar, cinnamon and 80 ml (2½ fl oz/⅓ cup) water in a saucepan over medium–high heat. Simmer, stirring regularly, for 25 minutes, or until the sauce is pulpy, with just a few chunks of apple left. Set aside until ready to serve.

When the pork is cooked, transfer to a serving dish and loosely cover with foil to keep it warm while it rests for 15 minutes. Don't skip the resting process as the meat needs to relax after being in the heat, allowing the juices to sink back through the meat, ensuring it is evenly juicy and tender. If you try to carve the meat before it has rested, the juices will run out and the meat will be dry.

While the pork is resting, make the gravy. Spoon off all but 2 tablespoons of pork fat from the roasting tin. Place the tin over one or two burners or stove hotplates over medium–high heat. Sprinkle the flour evenly over the surface and mix in with a wooden spoon. Using a balloon whisk, gradually whisk in the hot stock until the gravy is smooth, scraping up any cooked-on bits. (A balloon whisk is more effective than a wooden spoon for eliminating lumps.) Whisking occasionally, cook the gravy for a few minutes, or until thickened to a light coating consistency. Whisk in any resting juices from the pork and season to taste.

Carve the pork and serve with the gravy and apple sauce on the side for everyone to help themselves.

Roast beef for Sunday dinner was a British foodie tradition that Australian beef-eaters were keen to keep — although it seems Yorkshire pudding, the traditional accompaniment, has been almost completely ignored outside Britain. Many of us have let the Sunday dinner tradition slip, but why not make Sunday night a special family night again, and every once in a while serve up something you know everyone will love: roast beef, perfectly pink and melt in the mouth.

roast beef
with horseradish cream

olive oil, for pan-frying

1.2 kg (2 lb 10 oz) rib eye roast (4-rack)

2 tablespoons wholegrain mustard

1 small handful of flat-leaf (Italian) parsley, chopped

3 garlic cloves, crushed

160 g (5¾ oz/2 cups) soft white breadcrumbs

30 g (1 oz) melted butter, plus 10 g (¼ oz) butter, extra

2 teaspoons dijon mustard

1½ tablespoons plain (all-purpose) flour

2 tablespoons red wine (preferably the one you'll be drinking with dinner!), optional

375 ml (13 fl oz/1½ cups) hot beef stock

HORSERADISH CREAM

2 tablespoons bottled grated horseradish

1½ teaspoons dijon mustard

2 teaspoons lemon juice

½ teaspoon caster (superfine) sugar

2 tablespoons pouring (whipping) cream, lightly whipped

ground white pepper, to taste

serves 6

Preheat the oven to 190°C (375°F/Gas 5). Heat a little olive oil over high heat in a large, heavy-based frying pan. Season the beef all over with salt and black pepper and brown well on all sides. Remove and place on a rack in a roasting tin.

Combine the wholegrain mustard, parsley, garlic, breadcrumbs and melted butter. Season to taste. Smear the dijon mustard over the beef, then pat the breadcrumb mixture evenly over the top. Pour 125 ml (4 fl oz/½ cup) water into the base of the roasting tin.

Roast the beef for 50 minutes for a rare result, 60 minutes for medium, and a further 5 minutes if you prefer it more well done. If the crust is browning too quickly, cover it loosely with foil.

While the beef is roasting, make the horseradish cream. Combine the horseradish, mustard, lemon juice and sugar until smooth. Fold through the whipped cream and season to taste with salt and ground white pepper. Refrigerate until ready to serve.

When the beef is cooked, transfer to a serving platter and loosely cover with foil to keep it warm while it rests for 10–15 minutes.

While the meat is resting, make the gravy. Place the roasting tin over one or two burners or stove hotplates over medium–high heat. Add the extra butter and allow to melt. Sprinkle the flour evenly over the surface and mix in with a wooden spoon, scraping up any cooked-on bits. Using a balloon whisk, gradually whisk in the wine, then the hot stock, until smooth. (A balloon whisk is more effective than a wooden spoon for eliminating lumps.) Whisking occasionally, cook the gravy for a few minutes, or until thickened to a light coating consistency. Whisk in any resting juices from the beef and season to taste.

Carve the beef and serve with the gravy and horseradish cream on the side for everyone to help themselves.

✳lasagne

BECHAMEL SAUCE

1 litre (35 fl oz/4 cups) milk

375 ml (13 fl oz/1¹/₂ cups) pouring (whipping) cream

2 bay leaves

1 small brown onion, cut in half

80 g (2³/₄ oz) butter

a pinch of ground nutmeg

40 g (1¹/₂ oz/¹/₃ cup) plain (all-purpose) flour

500 g (1 lb 2 oz/3¹/₃ cups) grated mozzarella cheese

180 g (6¹/₂ oz/1³/₄ cups) grated parmesan cheese

butter, for greasing

2 x 250 g (9 oz) packets of instant lasagne sheets

1 quantity of bolognese sauce (see page 159)

serves 8–10

Preheat the oven to 190°C (375°F/Gas 5). To make the béchamel sauce, put the milk, cream, bay leaves and onion halves in a saucepan. Allow the liquid to just come to the boil, then immediately take the pan off the heat. Set aside to infuse for 15 minutes, then gently reheat before discarding the onion and bay leaves.

Melt the butter in a saucepan over medium–high heat, then add the nutmeg and flour and stir for 1 minute. Gradually whisk in the hot milk. Continue whisking for 5 minutes, or until the sauce is smooth and has thickened slightly. Remove from the heat and season to taste. Cover to keep warm.

Combine the cheeses. Liberally grease the base and sides of a 30 x 27 cm (12 x 10³/₄ inch) non-metallic baking dish with butter. Line with a layer of lasagne sheets — you may need to break a few pieces so they make a neat fit — then top with half the bolognese sauce. Top with another layer of lasagne sheets, then pour over half the béchamel sauce and sprinkle with a third of the cheese mixture. Add another layer of lasagne sheets, then cover with the remaining bolognese, followed by another layer of lasagne sheets. Pour the remaining béchamel sauce over the top and carefully spread it out to cover well. Sprinkle the remaining cheese mixture evenly over the top.

Bake for 1 hour, or until the topping is dark golden and bubbling and the lasagne sheets are tender when pierced with a sharp knife. Remove from the oven and allow to rest for 10 minutes. Serve with a crisp green salad.

After World War II, Italian immigrant families moved to many shores, sharing with their new homelands their rich heritage and amazing cuisine. One of the most loved of all Italian dishes is lasagne, the most popular version being luscious lasagne bolognese, which incorporates the bolognese sauce from page 159 with layers of pasta or lasagna sheets, béchamel sauce and freshly grated parmesan cheese. Sure, it takes some time to prepare — but it's still quicker than a trip to Italy...

Although the original version of bolognese sauce — or more correctly, 'ragu alla bolognese' — hails from Bologna, Italy, and is traditionally served with tagliatelle rather than spaghetti, spaghetti bolognese has become an essential (if inauthentic) dish in the basic repertoires of many households. I was never a huge fan of it when I was growing up, but in my adulthood I have enjoyed the pleasure of a few excellent versions, including one not so very long ago when a friend's Italian mother brought me a batch she had simmered for eight hours — it was incredible. Too often the sauce isn't cooked long enough and ends up watery and lacking in flavour. Now I'm not suggesting you chain yourself to the kitchen for a whole day, but please do cook your sauce for at least the time given in my recipe — and if you do have the time, cook it a bit longer, adding a little more of the liquid ingredients when you start. Truly, the flavour and fine texture is worth the wait.

spaghetti bolognese

2 tablespoons olive oil

1 brown onion, chopped

100 g (3½ oz) pancetta, finely chopped

1 large carrot, very finely chopped

1 large celery stalk, very finely chopped

4 garlic cloves, finely chopped

700 g (1 lb 9 oz) well-marbled minced (ground) beef

300 g (10½ oz) minced (ground) pork

250 ml (9 fl oz/1 cup) white wine (or red wine if you prefer a deeper flavour)

2 teaspoons finely chopped thyme

1 handful of oregano leaves, finely chopped

a good pinch of freshly ground nutmeg

90 g (3¼ oz/⅓ cup) tomato paste (concentrated purée)

2 x 400 g (14 oz) tins chopped tomatoes

500 ml (17 fl oz/2 cups) beef stock

¼ teaspoon sugar

500 g (1 lb 2 oz) spaghetti, tagliatelle or fettucine

freshly grated or shaved parmesan cheese, to serve

serves 6

Heat 1 tablespoon of the oil in a large saucepan over medium–high heat. Add the onion, pancetta, carrot and celery and sauté for 10 minutes, or until golden. Add the garlic and cook for 1 minute, then remove the mixture from the pan and set aside.

Add the remaining oil to the pan and brown the mince well in batches — it should take about 5 minutes per batch. Set aside with the vegetable mixture.

Add the wine to the pan and bring to the boil. Add the thyme, oregano, nutmeg, tomato paste, chopped tomatoes, stock, sugar and 500 ml (17 fl oz/2 cups) water. Mix well, then stir in the mince and vegetable mixture. Bring to the boil, reduce the heat and simmer for 4 hours, or until the sauce is rich and the meat is very tender. Season to taste.

Bring a large saucepan of lightly salted water to the boil. Add the pasta and cook according to the packet instructions, or until *al dente*. Drain and rinse briefly with cold water.

Serve the pasta topped with the bolognese sauce, with a small bowl of parmesan cheese on the side for sprinkling over.

VARIATION: Try adding some finely chopped porcini mushrooms or chicken livers to the sauce when you add the chopped tomatoes and stock. For an authentic touch, finish with a little cream in the last 15 minutes of cooking.

�֎ *Before you run, hear me out! I suspect most people enjoyed their mother's version of apricot chicken much more than they would care to admit, so I simply had to include a version of this sweet and savoury stew. However, my rendition more closely resembles a chicken and apricot tagine than the recipes from my childhood, which inevitably included the obligatory packet of French onion soup mix!*

apricot chicken

12 chicken drumsticks (about 2 kg/4 lb 8 oz in total)
2 tablespoons olive oil
1 large brown onion, diced
1 large carrot, diced
1 celery stalk, diced
2 garlic cloves, very finely chopped
2 teaspoons very finely chopped fresh ginger
1½ teaspoons ground cinnamon
2 teaspoons ground cumin
750 ml (26 fl oz/3 cups) chicken stock
180 g (6½ oz/1 cup) dried apricot halves
1 tablespoon honey
1 handful of coriander (cilantro) leaves, chopped
25 g (1 oz/¼ cup) toasted flaked almonds, to garnish, optional

serves 6

Lightly season the chicken drumsticks. Heat half the olive oil in a large, heavy-based saucepan or flameproof casserole dish over medium–high heat. Working in batches, brown the drumsticks well on all sides, adding a little more oil as needed. Remove from the pan and set aside.

Add the onion, carrot and celery to the pan and sauté for 10 minutes, or until golden. Add the garlic, ginger, cinnamon and cumin and cook for 30 seconds, or until fragrant. Put the drumsticks back in the pan and toss to coat. Add the stock, 250 ml (9 fl oz/1 cup) water, two-thirds of the apricots and the honey. Bring to the boil, then reduce the heat, cover and simmer for 35 minutes, or until the chicken is just cooked through and tender. Remove the chicken and cover to keep warm. Add the remaining apricots to the sauce and bring to the boil. Cook for 20 minutes, or until the sauce has thickened and is slightly glazy. Return the chicken to the pan with most of the coriander. Stir to coat the chicken and season to taste.

Serve, sprinkled with the flaked almonds, if using, and the remaining coriander. Great with couscous, rice or mashed potato.

chapter five *posh DINNERS

THIS CHAPTER GATHERS TOGETHER THE FOOD WE OFTEN SERVED AT DINNER PARTIES BACK IN THE 60S, 70S AND 80S WHEN TRYING TO IMPRESS — WHETHER FOR A BIRTHDAY SURPRISE, ROMANTIC DINNER FOR TWO, WOWING THE BOSS OR SIMPLY ENTERTAINING GOOD FRIENDS. THE MEALS OFTEN DREW UPON RICH AND DECADENT INGREDIENTS, NOT ONLY BECAUSE THEY WERE DELICIOUS BUT PERHAPS IN A CHEEKY DISPLAY OF AFFLUENCE! MENUS OFTEN INCLUDED FRENCH-INFLUENCED SAUCES MADE WITH BUTTER, CREAM AND CHEESE, EXTRAVAGANT SEAFOOD CONCOCTIONS AND PRIME CUTS OF MEATS.

WHEN WE STARTED BECOMING A LITTLE MORE HEALTH CONSCIOUS, MANY OF THESE FOODS BEGAN TO DISAPPEAR FROM THE MENU — BUT IF YOU EAT WELL ON A DAY-TO-DAY BASIS IT IS OKAY TO INDULGE ONCE IN A WHILE, SO WHY NOT TRY SOMETHING YOU HAVEN'T EATEN FOR YEARS BUT USED TO ADORE? AND IF YOU HAVEN'T TRIED THESE DISHES BEFORE BECAUSE YOU WERE TOO YOUNG THE FIRST TIME AROUND — FIND A SPECIAL OCCASION AND TREAT YOURSELF TO SOMETHING OLD THAT IS NEW AGAIN.

* oysters with chardonnay vinaigrette * prawn cocktail * cheese soufflé * coquilles st jacques * beef stroganoff * rack of lamb with minted pea purée & red wine jus * duck a l'orange * surf & turf * poached salmon with anchovy hollandaise * coq au vin * chicken kiev * steak diane * strawberries romanoff * peach melba

Often considered a daring or exotic food with a reputation as an aphrodisiac, oysters have never really gone out of fashion. Exquisitely briny and lusciously creamy, the very best and freshest are served 'au naturel' with a squeeze of lemon, but over the years some popular versions have emerged. From kilpatrick to mornay, steamed oysters and shooters, there is an oyster for everyone.

oysters with chardonnay vinaigrette

CHARDONNAY VINAIGRETTE
2 French shallots, very finely chopped
1½ tablespoons chardonnay
1½ tablespoons chardonnay vinegar
½ teaspoon honey
1 teaspoon dijon mustard
1 tablespoon macadamia nut oil
⅛ teaspoon pure vanilla extract

best-quality butter, for spreading
6 slices of wholemeal (whole-wheat) bread
baby cress, to garnish
24 Pacific oysters, on the half-shell

serves 4 as a starter

Put all the chardonnay vinaigrette ingredients in a small bowl and whisk until smooth. Season to taste. Allow to sit for about 20 minutes for the flavours to develop.

Butter the bread on one side, then top three slices with some baby cress. Cover with the remaining slices to form three sandwiches. Remove the crusts, then cut each sandwich into four triangles.

Top the oysters with a little chardonnay vinaigrette and garnish with a little cress. Serve six oysters per person, with three triangle sandwiches each. Serve immediately.

prawn cocktail

The prawn cocktail is a stayer — since the 60s it has come and gone many times, but never for too long as there is just 'something' about it ... There have been numerous reinventions and variations over the years, but a simple prawn cocktail should not be tampered with too much. Having said that, the original version might have got the flavours right, but the presentation of prawns mixed with dressing over shredded iceberg lettuce served in a coupe dish, as commonly found in club dining rooms, is a little outdated. My version is a bit more relaxed — but who knows what will be back in fashion by the time you are reading this?

DRESSING

60 g (2¼ oz/¼ cup) good-quality whole-egg mayonnaise

1 tablespoon plus 1 teaspoon tomato sauce (ketchup)

3 teaspoons horseradish cream

¾ teaspoon worcestershire sauce

1 teaspoon lemon juice

a few drops of Tabasco sauce

1½ teaspoons Cognac or brandy

1 tablespoon pouring (whipping) cream

a very small handful of chervil, finely chopped

1 baby cos (romaine) lettuce

12 cooked king (jumbo) prawns (shrimp)

1 ripe avocado

2 teaspoons lemon juice

1 Lebanese (short) cucumber

lemon cheeks, to serve

serves 4 as a starter

Put all the dressing ingredients in a bowl and whisk until smooth. Season to taste and refrigerate until ready to serve.

Trim off the very root end of the lettuce, then cut into quarters lengthways, keeping each quarter held together at the base. Refrigerate until ready to serve. Peel and devein the prawns, leaving the tails intact, and refrigerate until ready to serve. Remove the stone from the avocado and cut the flesh lengthways into quarters. Gently toss with the lemon juice and refrigerate. Slice the cucumber on the diagonal into long, elongated ovals and refrigerate.

To serve, arrange a lettuce quarter, avocado quarter, a few cucumber slices and three prawns on each serving plate. Dollop the dressing over the prawns, or serve in a small glass beaker for pouring or spooning over. Serve with the lemon cheeks.

VARIATION: Shred the lettuce, dice the avocado and cucumber, and layer them in a glass with the prawns arranged on top.

cheese soufflé

Ah, the soufflé — another scary dish many people are afraid to cook, but it really is quite simple as long as you are light-handed and follow the instructions closely. The most important thing is to have all your ingredients at hand prior to cooking, and to only cook the soufflé when you are ready to serve it as it will, no matter what you do, deflate quickly. A popular dish from eighteenth-century France, the soufflé enjoyed a renaissance in the 60s and still pops up in restaurant menus. There are so many wonderful cheeses available today, why not try a fantastically full-flavoured cheddar or perhaps some creamy goat's cheese for variation?

270 ml (9½ fl oz/1 cup plus 1 tablespoon) milk
½ brown onion, chopped
1 clove
1 bay leaf
½ teaspoon peppercorns
¼ teaspoon salt
60 g (2¼ oz) butter
40 g (1½ oz/⅓ cup) plain (all-purpose) flour, sifted
a large pinch of nutmeg
120 g (4¼ oz/1½ cups lightly packed) grated
    full-flavoured, mixed cheeses including parmesan,
    gruyère, blue cheese or sharp cheddar
4 large eggs, separated

serves 4–6

Preheat the oven to 200°C (400°F/Gas 6). Lightly grease a 1 litre (35 fl oz/4-cup capacity) soufflé dish with butter. Place a baking tray in the oven while the oven is heating.

Put the milk, onion, clove, bay leaf, peppercorns and salt in a saucepan and slowly bring to the boil. Remove from the heat and allow to infuse for 15 minutes. Strain.

Melt the butter in a clean saucepan over medium heat, then stir in the sifted flour and nutmeg until smooth. Cook for 1 minute, then gradually whisk in the strained milk and keep whisking until smooth and thick. Remove from the heat and stir in the cheese until melted. Set aside to cool slightly, then beat in the egg yolks until well combined.

Beat the egg whites using electric beaters until firm peaks form. Fold a large spoonful into the sauce, then carefully fold in the remaining egg white until just combined. Hold a large spoon, rounded side up, very close to the prepared soufflé dish, and pour the soufflé mixture over the back of the spoon to help break the fall so less air is lost from the mixture. The mixture should come almost to the top of the dish — if not, it won't rise properly.

Place the soufflé on the preheated baking tray and cook without opening the oven door for 25 minutes, or until puffed and golden. Remove from the oven and serve immediately as the soufflé will begin to deflate almost as soon as it hits the air. This rich soufflé is lovely served with a fresh little salad of sliced crisp apple, walnuts and baby green leaves or fresh herbs such as oregano or parsley.

NOTE: You can also use four individual 250 ml (9 fl oz/1 cup) soufflé dishes — the soufflés will only take 12–14 minutes to cook.

Beautifully sweet, plump scallops are often enjoyed simply grilled with some lemon or a light vinaigrette — but for something more decadent, try this rich, irresistible starter, which became very popular in the 70s. Coquilles St Jacques is French for 'the shell of St Jacques' or St James, and although commonly thought to be the name of this particular dish, it is in fact a generic term for scallops.

coquilles st jacques

12 large white scallops, on the shell
2 teaspoons olive oil
40 g (1½ oz) butter
3 French shallots, finely sliced
4 button mushrooms, sliced
1 garlic clove, very finely chopped
3 teaspoons plain (all-purpose) flour
2 tablespoons dry white wine
60 ml (2 fl oz/¼ cup) fish or chicken stock
125 ml (4 fl oz/½ cup) pouring (whipping) cream
1 bay leaf
2 teaspoons lemon juice
1 egg yolk
1 small handful of flat-leaf (Italian) parsley or
   chervil, finely chopped
65 g (2¼ oz/½ cup) finely grated gruyère cheese
15 g (½ oz/¼ cup) large Japanese breadcrumbs
   (panko), or large home-made breadcrumbs from
   a loaf of white bread that is several days old

serves 4

Using a small, sharp knife, carefully remove the scallops from their shells. Wash the shells well and dry, then set aside. Remove any hard muscle or membrane from the scallops, then toss the scallops with enough of the olive oil just to coat.

Heat a large, heavy-based frying pan over high heat. Season the scallops with a little salt, then sear quickly on each side for about 10 seconds, or just until coloured. Remove from the pan and place back onto each shell.

Reduce the heat to medium and add 1 tablespoon of the butter to the pan. When the butter has melted, sauté the shallot, mushroom and garlic for 6–8 minutes, or until the mushroom releases its liquid and it has evaporated off. Remove and set aside.

Add the remaining butter to the pan. When it has melted, sprinkle the flour over and stir until smooth. Whisk in the wine and cook for 1 minute. Whisk in the stock and then the cream until smooth. Add the bay leaf and lemon juice and stir continuously until the sauce boils and thickens. Add the shallot and mushroom mixture with the egg yolk, parsley and 2 tablespoons of the cheese and stir to combine. Remove from the heat and season to taste.

Preheat the grill (broiler) to medium–high. Remove the bay leaf from the sauce, then spoon the sauce over the scallops in their shells. Combine the breadcrumbs with the remaining cheese and evenly divide over the top of the scallops. Grill for 5 minutes, or until golden on top and just heated through. Serve three scallop shells per person on a plate with a small fork.

NOTE: You can serve the same sauce over lobster for a main course reminiscent of lobster thermidore.

beef stroganoff

750 g (1 lb 10 oz) piece of beef eye fillet
1½ tablespoons olive oil
60 g (2¼ oz) butter
1 large brown onion, sliced
250 g (9 oz) Swiss brown mushrooms, sliced
3 garlic cloves, crushed
60 ml (2 fl oz/¼ cup) Cognac or brandy
2 tablespoons tomato paste (concentrated purée)
435 ml (15¼ fl oz/1¾ cups) beef stock
3 teaspoons dijon mustard
300 g (10½ oz/1¼ cups) sour cream
chopped dill or parsley, to serve

serves 4–6

Cut the beef into strips 1 cm (½ inch) thick, 2 cm (¾ inch) wide and 5 cm (2 inches) long.

Heat 1 tablespoon of the olive oil and half the butter in a large, deep-sided, heavy-based frying pan over high heat. Season the beef strips with salt and freshly cracked black pepper and, working in small batches, sear the strips quickly to lightly brown them all over. Remove from the pan, cover and set aside.

Reduce the heat to medium–high and add the remaining olive oil. Add the onion and sauté for 5 minutes, or until softened and lightly golden. Add the remaining butter, mushroom and a large pinch of salt and cook for a further 5 minutes, or until the mushroom is slightly tender. Add the garlic and cook for a further 30 seconds. Remove the mixture from the pan and set aside.

Carefully pour the Cognac into the pan, scraping up any cooked-on bits. Add the tomato paste and cook for 1 minute, then whisk in the stock and mustard until smooth. Add the mushroom mixture and bring to the boil, then reduce the heat and simmer for 18–20 minutes, or until the sauce has thickened considerably.

Take a little of the hot sauce and whisk it into the sour cream until the mixture is lump free. Add the cream mixture to the pan with any resting juices from the meat and stir until smooth. Allow to simmer for a couple of minutes to thicken up again, then add the beef strips and cook for 2 minutes, or just until heated through.

Season to taste and serve with cooked pasta or egg noodles, tossed with a little butter and chopped dill or parsley. Beef stroganoff can also be served with fried potato straws, mashed potatoes or rice.

Said to have been invented several centuries ago by a chef to wealthy Russian aristocrats, the Stroganov family, this special-occasion dish is rich and luxurious and so very delicious — no wonder it became popular with beef-lovers back in the 1950s. The trick is to use excellent-quality beef and not to overcook it — the idea is to brown the meat first, then only gently reheat it in the sauce before serving.

It doesn't appear that the rack of lamb will ever go out of style, and it doesn't take a rocket scientist to work out why: the meat from the rack is so very succulent and delicious. And it has its own handles — a rather unique feature! I am salivating just thinking of tucking into some perfectly seared cutlets, but it would be very sad to miss out on the accompanying delectably modern version of 'minted peas'. The rich red wine jus with a hint of honey adds a subtle sweetness, bringing the whole dish together.

rack of lamb
with minted pea purée &
red wine jus

RED WINE JUS

375 ml (13 fl oz/1½ cups) lamb or chicken stock
250 ml (9 fl oz/1 cup) shiraz
1 mint sprig
4 garlic cloves, bruised
2 teaspoons honey

MINTED PEA PURÉE

1 large floury potato (about 200 g/7 oz), diced
500 g (1 lb 2 oz/3¼ cups) fresh or thawed frozen peas
40 g (1½ oz) butter
80 ml (2½ fl oz/⅓ cup) pouring (whipping) cream
a pinch of nutmeg
1 teaspoon sea salt flakes
1 small handful of mint leaves, very finely chopped

2 x 8-racks of lamb, French trimmed
olive oil, for rubbing

serves 4

Combine all the red wine jus ingredients in a saucepan and bring to the boil. Reduce the heat and simmer for 1½ hours, or until syrupy. Strain through a fine sieve, pressing on the solids to extract as much liquid as possible. Season to taste and cover to keep warm.

Meanwhile, preheat the oven to 190°C (375°F/Gas 5) and prepare the pea purée. Put the potato in a saucepan and cover with water. Bring to the boil and cook for 5 minutes, then add the peas, bring to the boil again and cook for a further 5 minutes, or until tender. Drain and place in a food processor or blender with the butter, cream, nutmeg and sea salt flakes and blend just until smooth. Return to the saucepan, stir in the mint and cover to keep warm.

Rub the lamb meat with a little olive oil, then sit the two lamb racks in a roasting tin and link the bones so they look like they are praying. Season with salt and pepper. Roast for 25–30 minutes for a medium–rare result; cook a little longer if you prefer your meat more well done. Remove from the oven, cover loosely with foil and allow to rest for 10 minutes. Meanwhile, gently reheat the red wine jus and the pea purée.

Carve each rack into cutlets. Tip any resting juices from the lamb into the red wine jus and allow to boil. Arrange the lamb cutlets on each plate and drizzle with the jus. Serve with the pea purée, and perhaps some golden roasted baby vegetables.

Duck and orange are a great team. While duck marries well with any sweet, slightly tart fruit, citrus is particularly wonderful for cutting through its richness — and let's face it, the French wouldn't have allowed this to become one of their most famous dishes without good reason. Duck a l'orange enjoyed great popularity in the 1950s, but you rarely find it anywhere these days. Many people are frightened to cook duck for fear it will dry out too much, but this slow-cooked method is foolproof, resulting in melt-in-the-mouth meat and the crispiest skin.

✳ duck a l'orange

2.5 kg (5 lb 8 oz) duck
1 small brown onion, cut in half
2 garlic cloves
1 small carrot, chopped
1 celery stalk, chopped
1 thyme sprig
1 bay leaf
3 teaspoons sea salt flakes

ORANGE SAUCE

1 tablespoon reserved duck fat
1½ tablespoons caster (superfine) sugar
1 tablespoon red wine vinegar
80 ml (2½ fl oz/⅓ cup) reserved cooking juices
   from the duck, or chicken stock
250 ml (9 fl oz/1 cup) strained, freshly squeezed
   orange juice
2 teaspoons julienned orange zest
2 teaspoons Grand Marnier, or other
   orange-flavoured liqueur
orange segments, optional

serves 4

Preheat the oven to 120°C (235°F/Gas ½). Remove the neck and giblets from the duck if still intact. Rinse the duck inside and out and pat dry. Discard the parson's nose and a small amount of the surrounding area to remove the oil glands. Insert the onion halves, garlic, carrot, celery, thyme and bay leaf into the cavity of the duck and seal with a skewer. Carefully prick the skin all over by inserting a thin skewer in and under the skin at an angle almost parallel to the duck, which will prevent the flesh being pierced. Rub the sea salt flakes all over the duck skin.

Place the duck, breast side up, on a 'v'-shaped rack in a roasting tin, and place the neck in the base of the tin. Tuck the wings under and roast for 2½ hours. There is no need to baste.

Remove the duck from the oven and increase the temperature to 200°C (400°F/Gas 6). Tip off the fat accumulated in the bottom of the tin. Reserve 1 tablespoon for the sauce. (Keep the rest for making the best roast potatoes! The strained duck fat will keep in the fridge for several months.) Pour 375 ml (13 fl oz/1½ cups) water into the roasting tin, then roast the duck for a further 1½ hours, or until crisp and deep golden all over. Remove from the oven, tip any liquid in the roasting tin into a jug, spoon off any fat when it settles and reserve 80 ml (2½ fl oz/⅓ cup) of the cooking liquid for the sauce. Cover the duck loosely with foil and allow to rest for 15 minutes.

While the duck is resting, make the orange sauce. Put the reserved duck fat in a small saucepan with the sugar and stir to combine. Bring to the boil over high heat and cook for 2 minutes, or until the sugar is deeply caramelized. Add the vinegar, reserved cooking juices, orange juice and orange zest. The sugar will solidify, but will dissolve again once the mixture comes to the boil. Cook for 10 minutes, then add any resting juices from the duck, bring to the boil again and cook for a further 5 minutes, or until glazy.

Take the sauce off the heat and add the liqueur and orange segments, if using. Gently shake the pan to warm through. Carve the duck and serve with the orange sauce spooned over. Wonderful with potatoes roasted in the leftover duck fat, with some lightly cooked green vegetables or a salad of bitter greens.

VARIATIONS: Instead of using orange segments, add some pitted fresh cherries to the sauce and gently cook until the fruit is tender and the sauce is coloured by the cherries. Grapes or blood orange are also lovely. Or soak some raisins or muscatels in hot water, then drain and add to the sauce with a splash of rich sherry. While it is traditional to use a whole duck for this dish, you could also use duck breast fillets, which have a much shorter cooking time.

✳ *Surf and turf was a popular choice at restaurants in the decadent 80s when one too many pre-meal champagnes hindered making decisions about the main course. Although this dish sounds excessive it can actually be quite superb. A combination of meats — usually fillet of beef or veal and your choice of shellfish — is finished with a rich, buttery bearnaise sauce, making it a dish for special occasions only (we're talking hips as well as hip pockets here)!*

surf & turf

4 x 120 g (4¼ oz) cooked balmain or moreton bay bugs
  (flat-head lobsters)
4 x 180 g (6½ oz) veal noisettes (see Note)
1 tablespoon olive oil
1 teaspoon butter
tarragon sprigs, to garnish, optional

**LEMON MUSTARD &
TARRAGON BEARNAISE**
125 ml (4 fl oz/½ cup) white wine
2 tablespoons tarragon vinegar
2 tablespoons lemon juice, plus ½ teaspoon, extra
4 French shallots, very finely chopped
½ teaspoon peppercorns
a few parsley stalks
3 egg yolks
2½ teaspoons dijon mustard
150 g (5½ oz) butter, diced & chilled
1 teaspoon finely chopped fresh tarragon

serves 4

Carefully remove the meat from the bug shells in one piece and refrigerate until 10 minutes before you are ready to serve.

To make the lemon mustard and tarragon bearnaise, put the wine, vinegar, lemon juice, shallot, peppercorns and parsley stalks in a saucepan and bring to the boil. Reduce the heat and simmer for 10 minutes, or until reduced to about 1 tablespoon of liquid. Strain into a bowl and cool slightly.

In a heatproof bowl, lightly beat the egg yolks with 1½ teaspoons of the mustard and whisk in the cooled liquid. Place the bowl over a saucepan of simmering water and whisk for 2 minutes, or until thickened slightly. Whisk in the butter, a few cubes at a time, adding more butter only after each cube is incorporated into the liquid. Whisk continuously until all the butter is added and the sauce is thick and glossy. This should take 8–10 minutes. Remove from the heat, whisk in the remaining mustard, the tarragon and the extra ½ teaspoon of lemon juice, season to taste and cover to keep warm. (If you wish to make the sauce in advance, refrigerate it until needed, then reheat very gently over a pan of simmering water, whisking continuously until just heated through — do not allow to overheat or the sauce will separate and become oily.)

Season the veal with salt and pepper. Heat the olive oil and butter in a large, heavy-based frying pan and cook the veal for 3 minutes on each side for a pink result. Remove from the pan, cover loosely with foil and set aside to rest for 5 minutes.

To serve, top the veal with the bug meat, then the bearnaise sauce. Garnish with a tarragon sprig. Great with lightly cooked greens such as sugar snap peas, snow peas (mangetout) and asparagus, or over some wilted spinach.

NOTE: Noisettes, also called medallions, are a small, tender fillet cut from the loin or rib. You could use veal cutlets or beef instead of veal fillets — adjust cooking times as necessary. You could also use yabbies, prawns (shrimp), lobster or crabmeat instead of the bugs.

Poached salmon was a big hit when I was cooking for boardroom lunches in the early 90s — particularly when the female partners were hosting. The boys consistently requested fillet of beef, so it was a refreshing change for me as well as the executives. This elegant dish, topped with fresh herbs and a buttery hollandaise, is perfect with tender asparagus spears and a glass of chardonnay — ooh la la!

poached salmon
with anchovy hollandaise

125 ml (4 fl oz/½ cup) white wine
a few parsley stalks
2 slices of lemon
1 teaspoon peppercorns
2 bay leaves
4 x 200 g (7 oz) skinless salmon fillets
4 tablespoons finely chopped chives
1 large handful of flat-leaf (Italian) parsley,
    very finely chopped
lemon cheeks, to serve, optional

ANCHOVY HOLLANDAISE
1 tablespoon lemon juice
2 egg yolks
2 small anchovies, very finely chopped
1 garlic clove, crushed
150 g (5½ oz) butter, chilled & cut into small dice
ground white pepper, for seasoning

serves 4

Put the wine, parsley stalks, lemon slices, peppercorns, bay leaves and 1 litre (35 fl oz/4 cups) water into a large, deep frying pan over high heat. Bring to the boil, then reduce the heat and allow the liquid to simmer for 10 minutes for the flavours to develop. Remove the solids with a slotted spoon.

While the poaching liquid is simmering, make the anchovy hollandaise. Whisk together the lemon juice, egg yolks, anchovy and garlic in a heatproof bowl and place over a pan of simmering water. Whisk until foamy, then whisk in a few cubes of the butter until incorporated into the egg mixture. Continue whisking until all the butter has been incorporated and the sauce has thickened. Remove from the heat and season to taste with salt and ground white pepper. Keep warm.

Add the salmon, rounded side down, to the simmering poaching liquid and cook for 2 minutes. Carefully turn the salmon over and cook for a further 2 minutes. Turn off the heat and allow the salmon to sit in the poaching liquid for 3–5 minutes, depending on the thickness of the fish and how you like it cooked. Remove with a fish lifter or wide, slotted spatula, then drain on a clean tea towel (dish towel) or paper towel.

Combine the herbs and sprinkle liberally and evenly over the rounded side of the salmon fillets, patting down slightly to help the herbs adhere. Serve the salmon herb side up, with a dollop of the hollandaise and some lemon cheeks for squeezing over, if desired. Wonderful with lightly cooked asparagus or English spinach, and perhaps some baby potatoes on the side.

This dish often made an appearance at dinner parties in the 70s and 80s — and if you knew how to pronounce it you were probably showing off! This classic French Burgundian festival dish, originally made with a rooster (coq) instead of a chicken, is simple to make, but lusciously rich and warming with the deep, smoky flavours of quality bacon, red wine, mushrooms and baby onions. Serve with some creamy mashed potato as a dressed-up comfort food when you want to impress with ease.

coq au vin

2 kg (4 lb 8 oz) chicken, cut into 8 pieces
1 tablespoon olive oil
1 tablespoon butter
125 g (4¹/₂ oz) piece of smoked bacon, cut into
  short strips about 1 cm (¹/₂ inch) wide
12 baby onions
1 large carrot, diced
1 large celery stalk, diced
200 g (7 oz) small button mushrooms
3 garlic cloves, finely chopped
60 ml (2 fl oz/¹/₄ cup) Cognac
750 ml (26 fl oz/3 cups) full-bodied red wine,
  such as Burgundy or cabernet sauvignon
375 ml (13 fl oz/1¹/₂ cups) brown chicken stock
  or veal stock
1 bouquet garni
1 bay leaf

1 tablespoon butter, extra, softened
1 tablespoon plain (all-purpose) flour
1 small handful of flat-leaf (Italian) parsley,
  finely chopped

serves 4–6

Season the chicken pieces with salt and a little freshly cracked black pepper. Heat the olive oil and half the butter in a large flameproof casserole dish over medium–high heat. Working in batches, brown the chicken pieces well all over — this should take about 5 minutes per batch. Set aside.

Add the bacon to the pan and sauté for 3 minutes, or until lightly browned. Set aside with the chicken. Add the onions, carrot and celery and sauté for 5 minutes, or until lightly golden. Set aside with the chicken.

Add the remaining butter to the pan with the mushrooms and garlic and cook for 3 minutes, or until the garlic is lightly coloured. Carefully pour in the Cognac and wine and stir to scrape up any cooked-on bits. Put the stock, bouquet garni, bay leaf, chicken and all the vegetables back in the pan and stir to combine. Bring just to the boil, then immediately reduce the heat to low. Simmer for 20–25 minutes, or until the chicken is just cooked through. (You may need to take the breast pieces out earlier as they will cook more quickly than the legs, and overcooking will only make them tough.) Remove all the chicken and cover to keep warm.

Increase the heat to high and bring the sauce to the boil. Continue to cook for 25 minutes to reduce the sauce slightly and concentrate the flavours, then remove the bouquet garni and bay leaf.

Combine the extra butter with the flour to form a smooth paste. Whisk a teaspoon of the paste at a time into the sauce until thickened slightly and glossy. Add the chicken and stir to coat. Cook for a few minutes, or until the chicken is just heated through. Stir in the parsley and season to taste. Serve with mashed potato.

✳ chicken kiev

HERB BUTTER

80 g (2¾ oz) butter, softened
4 garlic cloves, crushed
1 teaspoon finely grated lemon zest
1 handful of flat-leaf (Italian) parsley, finely chopped
3 teaspoons chopped dill
a pinch of cayenne pepper
1 teaspoon sea salt flakes

4 x 200–220 g (7–7¾ oz) boneless, skinless
   chicken breasts
40 g (1½ oz/⅓ cup) plain (all-purpose) flour, seasoned
   well with salt & pepper
4 eggs, lightly beaten
320 g (11¼ oz/4 cups) fresh white breadcrumbs
olive oil, for deep-frying
lemon wedges, to serve

serves 4

Put all the herb butter ingredients in a bowl and mix until thoroughly combined. Divide into four equal portions, then roll each into a log about 7 cm (2¾ inches) long. Wrap each log individually in plastic wrap and freeze until firm.

Using a long, sharp knife, cut into the chicken breasts through the side, using a slight sawing action until you almost reach the opposite side of the breast — be careful not to cut right through. Open up each breast at the hinge and place between two pieces of plastic wrap. Without allowing it to tear, beat with a meat mallet or rolling pin until as thin as possible — preferably about 5 mm (¼ inch) thick. Trim the very edges to make a vague rectangle.

Unwrap the herb butter and place a log across one shorter end of each chicken fillet. Roll it up like a spring roll, folding in the sides along the way. The butter should be well covered by the chicken to ensure it does not escape.

Lightly coat the chicken in the seasoned flour. Dip into the beaten egg, allowing any excess to drip off, before pressing both sides of the breast into the breadcrumbs to help them adhere. Repeat with the egg and breadcrumbs to double-coat the chicken, which helps prevent the butter leaking out. Refrigerate for 1 hour for the crumbs to set.

Fill a deep-fryer or large, heavy-based saucepan one-third full of olive oil and heat to 170°C (325°F), or until a cube of bread dropped into the oil browns in 20 seconds. Cook the first two kievs for 10–12 minutes, or until the crumbs are deep golden and the chicken is just cooked through. Keep warm in a low oven while cooking the remaining two kievs.

Serve hot with lemon wedges on the side for squeezing over. Lovely with mashed or baby potatoes and a crisp green salad.

VARIATION: Don't be afraid to change the flavours in the herb butter by adding your own favourite herbs or spices.

Although not a Russian invention as the name might suggest, the kiev, invented by a French chef, did become popular in Ukranian restaurants after World War II. In the 1980s it was also a favourite in our house (albeit an expensive one). Luckily our local gourmet chicken shop had an endless freshly made supply so we could simply take it home and cook it — no preparation needed. As with most fashionable items, the kiev's popularity has fluctuated and it isn't so easy to find nowadays — except perhaps in the supermarket freezer, which will of course taste nothing like this home-made version. Fortunately, it really isn't difficult to make once you get the hang of butterflying the chicken. It's great for dinner parties, but you best make extra as kids love this one too.

✳ Although it was immensely popular during the 50s, 60s and 70s, finding an authentic recipe for steak diane is almost impossible as the origins of the sauce are hazy to say the least. However, it's likely to be an adaptation of a very rich French game sauce containing lots of pepper, truffles and cream, prepared in honour of Diana, goddess of hunting. Search through recipe books or the internet and you won't find two recipes the same, so my version is how I remember it. If the only diane sauce you have ever eaten is out of a packet, give this a go and there will be no turning back.

steak diane

4 x 200 g (7 oz) beef fillets

1 tablespoon olive oil

30 g (1 oz) butter

3 French shallots, finely chopped

2 garlic cloves, very finely chopped

60 ml (2 fl oz/¼ cup) Cognac

1 tablespoon plus 1 teaspoon worcestershire sauce

2 teaspoons dijon mustard

125 ml (4 fl oz/½ cup) rich beef stock or demi-glace
(available at good butchers & speciality stores —
or make your own beef stock & reduce until
slightly glazy)

125 ml (4 fl oz/½ cup) pouring (whipping) cream

½ teaspoon lemon juice

1 small handful of flat-leaf (Italian) parsley,
finely chopped

serves 4

Cut the beef fillets in half through the middle to form eight thin steaks. Season the beef on both sides with salt and plenty of freshly cracked black pepper. Heat the olive oil in a large, heavy-based frying pan over high heat. Cook the steaks for 2 minutes on each side for a medium–rare result. Remove from the pan and cover to keep warm.

Reduce the heat to medium and add the butter to the pan with the shallot. Cook for 1 minute, or until softened. Add the garlic and cook for 30 seconds. Carefully pour in the Cognac and allow to boil, then add the worcestershire sauce, mustard and stock. Stir until smooth. Stir in the cream, increase the heat to high and bring to the boil again. Cook for 6 minutes, or until thickened slightly.

Stir in the lemon juice and any resting juices from the steaks. Add the parsley and season to taste. Serve immediately over the rested steaks. Terrific with fried or boiled potatoes and lightly cooked green vegetables.

A simple but heavenly dessert, this fancy version of strawberries and cream, popular at dinner parties in the 70s, was the creation of the great French pastry chef Marie-Antoine Carême in the 1800s. I will never forget being introduced to this strawberry-scented cloud of a dessert at a posh neighbourhood restaurant as a child — it certainly made up for the fact I never owned one of those sweet-smelling Strawberry Shortcake dolls!

strawberries
romanoff

500 g (1 lb 2 oz/3$\frac{1}{3}$ cups) small, ripe strawberries, hulled & cut in half

80 ml (2$\frac{1}{2}$ fl oz/$\frac{1}{3}$ cup) orange-flavoured liqueur, such as Cointreau or Grand Marnier

1 tablespoon icing (confectioners') sugar, plus extra for sprinkling, optional

330 ml (11$\frac{1}{4}$ fl oz/1$\frac{1}{3}$ cups) pouring (whipping) cream

80 g (2$\frac{3}{4}$ oz/$\frac{1}{3}$ cup) caster (superfine) sugar

1$\frac{1}{4}$ teaspoons pure vanilla extract

toasted flaked almonds, to garnish

serves 6

Gently toss the strawberries with the liqueur and icing sugar, then refrigerate for 2–4 hours — any longer and the strawberries will start to become mushy.

Put the cream, caster sugar and vanilla in a bowl and whip to medium–firm peaks.

Divide the strawberries and accumulated juices among six glass serving dishes or glasses. Top with the whipped cream, then garnish with the toasted flaked almonds. Sift a little extra icing sugar over the top if desired.

NOTE: You can use strained, freshly squeezed orange juice instead of the liqueur, or half juice and half liqueur.

What's a posh dinner without a posh dessert? I've used a lot of artistic licence here. The original recipe — developed by French chef Auguste Escoffier to honour a visit by Australian opera singer Dame 'Nellie' Melba in the 1800s — was simply a poached peach with raspberry sauce and vanilla ice cream served in meringue swan wings. I have translated it into a modern dessert of vanilla bean panna cotta with crushed raspberries and poached peaches in an intense peachy syrup. Superb!

peach melba

RASPBERRY CRUSH
150 g (5½ oz/1¼ cups) raspberries
2 tablespoons raspberry liqueur
icing (confectioners') sugar, to taste

VANILLA PANNA COTTA
500 ml (17 fl oz/2 cups) pouring (whipping) cream
1 vanilla bean, split lengthways & seeds scraped
55 g (2 oz/¼ cup) caster (superfine) sugar
2½ teaspoons powdered gelatine

POACHED PEACHES
115 g (4 oz/½ cup) caster (superfine) sugar
½ vanilla bean
1 teaspoon grated lemon zest
3 small ripe, firm peaches

serves 4

To make the raspberry crush, put the raspberries in a small bowl and crush with the back of a spoon. Stir in the liqueur and icing sugar, to taste. Spoon into four freezer-proof 375 ml (13 fl oz/ 1½ cup) glasses or small glass bowls and place in the freezer.

To make the vanilla panna cotta, put the cream, vanilla bean, vanilla seeds and sugar in a saucepan over medium–high heat and stir until the sugar has dissolved. Bring just to the boil, then reduce the heat and simmer for 5 minutes. Remove from the heat and allow to infuse for 20 minutes.

Put the cream mixture back over medium heat. Bring just to the boil again and remove from the heat. Pour 60 ml (2 fl oz/¼ cup) of the hot cream mixture into a small bowl and sprinkle the gelatine over the top. Wait until it becomes spongy, then whisk until smooth with a fork. Pour back into the rest of the hot cream mixture and stir until the gelatine has completely dissolved. Strain into a jug and allow to cool to room temperature.

Remove the raspberry crush from the freezer and pour the panna cotta mixture over the top. Cover and refrigerate for 3 hours to set the panna cotta — it should still be a little wobbly.

To poach the peaches, put the sugar, vanilla bean, lemon zest and 500 ml (17 fl oz/2 cups) water in a saucepan. Stir over high heat until the sugar has dissolved and bring to the boil. Meanwhile, cut the peaches in half and reserve the stones. Cut each peach half into four slices. Add the peach slices and stones to the boiling liquid, allow the mixture to come to the boil again, then reduce the heat and simmer for 30 minutes, or until the peach slices are tender.

Remove the peach slices with a slotted spoon to cool a little, leaving the stones in the pan to simmer (they will flavour the syrup). Peel the peaches and add only the skins to the pan. Bring the liquid to the boil again and cook for 10–12 minutes, or until the sauce has thickened and is slightly syrupy. Strain the syrup over the peach slices, allow to cool slightly, then refrigerate until cold.

To serve, spoon some peach slices and syrup over the panna cotta.

chapter six *NANNA'S PUDS

STICKY, SILKY, GOOEY, WARM AND FILLING: LUSCIOUS ENDINGS TO A HOME-COOKED MEAL THAT MADE YOU FEEL CONTENT AND PERHAPS A LITTLE SLEEPY, OR TIPPED YOU OVER THE EDGE WITH THAT EXTRA SERVING. SINCE THE DAWN OF TIME GRANDMAS HAVE BEEN ALLOWED TO SPOIL THE FAMILY — THEY HAVE FILLED THEIR QUOTA OF RESPONSIBLE PARENTING AND NOW REJOICE IN THE CHANCE TO REBEL AND SNEAK A LITTLE EXTRA ON YOUR PLATE OR SLIP A SWEET INTO YOUR HAND WHEN NO-ONE IS LOOKING. BUT YOU DON'T HAVE TO BE A NANNA TO INDULGE IN THE CATHARTIC PROPERTIES OF PREPARING SOMETHING YOU KNOW EVERYONE WILL LOVE!

THIS PERSONAL COLLECTION OF RECIPES FEATURES CLASSIC DESSERTS THAT HAVE INDEED BEEN PASSED DOWN FROM GRANDPARENT TO PARENT TO CHILD, SO IF YOU DON'T HAVE YOUR OWN TREASURED RECIPES FOR THE TREATS YOU ENJOYED IN YOUR EARLIER YEARS, PLEASE SHARE MINE AND START THE BALL ROLLING AGAIN — YOUR OWN FRIENDS, RELATIVES AND DESCENDANTS WILL THANK YOU.

---

* lemon & rhubarb meringue pie * baked brown sugar custard with dates * creamed rice * apple, rhubarb & strawberry crumble * lemon delicious * coconut & mandarin golden syrup dumplings * macadamia treacle tart * chocolate malted self-saucing pudding * pavlova with mango cream * bread & butter pudding * baked banana cheesecake * trifle * banana fritters with caramel rum sauce * sticky date pudding

---

❋ lemon & rhubarb meringue pie

3 sheets of ready-made shortcrust (pie) pastry, or
  1 quantity of treacle tart pastry (see page 204),
  rolled out to 3 mm (1/8 inch)

FILLING
30 g (1 oz/1/4 cup) plain (all-purpose) flour
1 tablespoon cornflour (cornstarch)
3 teaspoons finely grated lemon zest
345 g (12 oz/1½ cups) caster (superfine) sugar
185 ml (6 fl oz/3/4 cup) lemon juice
6 large egg yolks
1 rhubarb stalk, trimmed & finely diced
60 g (2¼ oz) unsalted butter, diced

MERINGUE
6 large egg whites
345 g (12 oz/1½ cups) caster (superfine) sugar
½ teaspoon natural vanilla extract
1 teaspoon cornflour (cornstarch)

makes 6 individual pies

Cut the pastry into six 15 cm (6 inch) circles. Fit them into the base of six lightly greased, 10 cm (4 inch) wide, 3 cm (1½ inch) deep, non-stick, fluted, loose-based flan (tartlet) tins. Trim the pastry edges and prick the bases with a fork. Refrigerate for 30 minutes.

Preheat the oven to 180°C (350°F/Gas 4). Line each pastry base with a lightly crumpled piece of baking paper and fill with baking beads, uncooked rice or dried beans. Place on a baking tray and bake for 15 minutes, then remove the paper and weights and bake for a further 5–10 minutes, or until the surface is dry and lightly golden. Remove the pastry from the oven and set aside to cool. Increase the oven temperature to 210°C (415°F/Gas 6–7).

While the pastry is baking, make the filling. Put the flour, cornflour, lemon zest and sugar in a saucepan. Gradually whisk in the combined lemon juice and 375 ml (13 fl oz/1½ cups) water. Place over medium–high heat and whisk continuously for 8–10 minutes, or until the mixture boils and thickens slightly. Reduce the heat and simmer for 3 minutes, stirring regularly, until thick and slightly gelatinous. Remove from the heat and allow to cool slightly.

Beat the egg yolks into the filling mixture, one at a time. Stir in the rhubarb. Place back over low heat and cook for 10 minutes, stirring constantly. Gradually beat in the butter, a few cubes at a time, until the butter is well incorporated and the mixture is glossy — this should take about 5 minutes. Allow to cool slightly, then spoon into the pie shells and leave to cool to room temperature.

To make the meringue, beat the egg whites and sugar using electric beaters until light and fluffy, then continue to beat on high for 12–15 minutes, or until stiff and glossy. Beat in the vanilla and cornflour until well combined.

Spread the meringue over each pie, piling it up high towards the centre. If you like, make small peaks all over with the back of a spoon. Put the pies on the baking tray and bake for 8 minutes, or until the meringue is lightly golden. Cool to room temperature on a wire rack, then carefully remove the pies from each tin and serve.

NOTE: You can make one large pie, using a 21 cm (8¼ inch) wide, 3 cm (1¼ inch) deep, fluted, loose-based flan (tart) tin. Cook the meringue for 12 minutes. If rhubarb is not in season, simply omit it and drop the sugar in the filling back to 285 g (10 oz/1¼ cups).

On too many occasions I remember pacing back and forth past the lemon meringue pie as it cooled by the kitchen window while we waited for dad to get home from the surf — heaven help us if we cut into his precious pie before he did! It was his absolute favourite. He loved lemons so much he would eat them straight from their skins, sprinkled with plenty of salt. This might sound strange considering he had such a sweet tooth, but salt actually brings out the sweetness of bitter foods. Above all though he adored the fluffy, sugary joy of lemon meringue pie.

This addictive European dessert dates back to the Middle Ages. The custard is delectably light and silky when served warm, but is also pretty wonderful the next day as it develops a dense, creamy texture upon cooling. Dates are available in various guises — make sure you buy the fresh, plump, slightly wrinkly ones from your greengrocer for the best results.

baked brown sugar custard with dates

10 fresh dates, pitted and cut in half
1 vanilla bean, split lengthways & seeds scraped
500 ml (17 fl oz/2 cups) pouring (whipping) cream
375 ml (13 fl oz/1½ cups) milk
10 large egg yolks
140 g (5 oz/¾ cup) soft brown sugar
fresh nutmeg, for grating

serves 6

Preheat the oven to 160°C (315°F/Gas 2–3). Grease an 8 cm (3½ inch) deep, 1.5–2 litre (52–70 fl oz/6–8-cup capacity), non-metallic baking dish. Evenly distribute the date halves around the bottom of the dish — it should be a neat fit.

Put the vanilla bean and seeds in a saucepan with the cream and milk over medium heat and slowly bring just to the boil. Remove from the heat, then cover and allow to infuse for 15 minutes.

Meanwhile, whisk the egg yolks and sugar together until smooth. Strain the infused milk mixture and gradually whisk it into the egg yolks until smooth. Carefully pour the mixture over the dates, trying not to disturb them. Finely grate enough nutmeg over the custard to lightly cover the surface.

Place the baking dish in a large roasting tin, then pour in enough warm water to come halfway up the side of the baking dish. Bake for 1½ hours, or until the custard is dry and golden on top but still a little wobbly.

Remove the baking dish from the oven, but leave it in the water bath for 10 minutes. Carefully lift the baking dish from the water bath and allow the custard to rest for a further 10 minutes, before serving on its own or with some lightly whipped cream.

NOTE: You can omit the dates altogether if you prefer.

This warming pudding is an English nursery school favourite, but creamed rice or rice puddings are enjoyed in many nations — Spain, Italy and Denmark, just to name a few. Usually served as a wintery dessert, it also makes a great breakfast when topped with juicy, ripe fruits. I have used Italian arborio rice here as it produces such a wonderful creamy texture, but you can substitute with any short-grained rice. Don't bother using long-grain rice as it doesn't contain enough starch to adequately thicken the sauce.

creamed rice

1.25 litres (44 fl oz/5 cups) milk
1 vanilla bean, split lengthways &
  seeds scraped
2 large strips of lemon or orange zest
220 g (7¾ oz/1 cup) arborio rice
145 g (5½ oz/⅔ cup) caster (superfine) sugar
ground cinnamon or nutmeg, for sprinkling

serves 6

Put the milk, vanilla bean, vanilla seeds and citrus zest in a saucepan and bring just to the boil. Turn off the heat and allow to infuse for 20 minutes. Add the rice and sugar, place back over high heat and cook, stirring continuously, until the sugar has completely dissolved. Reduce the heat and simmer, stirring regularly, for 45 minutes, or until the rice is tender but not mushy. Remove the zest and vanilla bean.

Serve lightly sprinkled with cinnamon or nutmeg, accompanied by the fruit of your choice — try poached fruits (such as peaches, apricots, plums), fresh cherries or seasonal berries.

VARIATIONS: Experiment by adding a variety of spices to the mixture (such as cardamom, ginger, bay leaf or star anise) — or add some lemon grass and lime zest to a batch and serve with ripe mangoes, bananas and toasted coconut, or a drizzle of passionfruit pulp. Add toasted nuts and dried fruits if you like. A few drops of rosewater or orange blossom water adds an exotic touch. You can even add some chopped dark chocolate at the end for chocoholics.

Who can resist a good crumble? In this version, tart rhubarb in the filling is balanced with luscious strawberries and apples, and is not overly sweet. The topping is a crumbly, crunchy combination of wholesome oats, coconut and toasty almonds, warmly spiced with ginger and cinnamon. Yum!

apple, rhubarb & strawberry crumble

600 g (1 lb 5 oz) trimmed rhubarb stalks
500 g (1 lb 2 oz/3⅓ cups) strawberries
2 granny smith apples
1½ teaspoons finely grated orange zest
230 g (8½ oz/1 cup) caster (superfine) sugar
2 tablespoons plain (all-purpose) flour

CRUMBLE TOPPING

185 g (6½ oz/1½ cups) plain (all-purpose) flour
½ teaspoon baking powder
1 teaspoon ground cinnamon
½ teaspoon ground ginger
95 g (3½ oz/½ cup) soft brown sugar
180 g (6½ oz) unsalted butter, diced
75 g (2¾ oz/¾ cup) rolled (porridge) oats
30 g (1 oz/½ cup) shredded coconut
60 g (2¼ oz/½ cup) slivered almonds

serves 6–8

Preheat the oven to 180°C (350°F/Gas 4). Liberally butter a wide, 6 cm (2½ inch) deep, 2–2.5 litre (70–87 fl oz/8–10-cup capacity) non-metallic baking dish.

Remove any fibrous strings from the rhubarb and cut the stalks into 3 cm (1¼ inch) pieces. Hull the strawberries and cut them in half. Peel and core the apples, then cut into 1½ cm (⅝ inch) dice. Put all the fruit in a bowl with the orange zest. Sprinkle the sugar and flour over the top and toss well so that all the fruit is evenly coated. Evenly distribute around the bottom of the baking dish.

To make the crumble topping, combine the flour, baking powder, cinnamon, ginger and sugar in a bowl. Rub the butter into the flour mixture until it forms rough crumbs. Stir in the rolled oats, coconut and slivered almonds. Evenly scatter the crumble mixture over the fruit.

Bake for 45–50 minutes, or until the filling is cooked and the topping is crisp and golden. If it is browning too quickly, cover the top loosely with foil. Remove from the oven and rest for 5 minutes before serving with ice cream, custard or cream.

lemon delicious

60 g (2¼ oz) unsalted butter, chopped
230 g (8½ oz/1 cup) caster (superfine) sugar
3 teaspoons finely grated lemon zest
4 eggs, separated
30 g (1 oz/¼ cup) self-raising flour
310 ml (10¾ fl oz/1¼ cups) milk
80 ml (2½ fl oz/⅓ cup) lemon juice
icing (confectioners') sugar, to serve, optional
whipped cream, to serve

serves 4

Preheat the oven to 180°C (350°F/Gas 4). Lightly grease a deep-sided, non-metallic 2 litre (70 fl oz/8-cup capacity) baking dish or soufflé dish.

Beat the butter, sugar and lemon zest using electric beaters until pale and creamy. With the motor still running, gradually add the egg yolks, beating well after each addition. Mix in the flour, then the milk, beating until smooth. Stir in the lemon juice. The mixture will look curdled at this point.

In a separate bowl, whisk the egg whites with a pinch of salt until firm peaks form. Fold a spoonful of the egg white into the cake batter, then gently fold in the remaining egg white, being careful not to beat out the air. Carefully pour the mixture into the prepared baking dish and sit it inside a large roasting tin. Pour in enough hot water to come halfway up the side of the baking dish.

Bake for 55–60 minutes, or until the top is deep golden and firm to the touch. Remove the baking dish from the oven, but leave it in the water bath for another 15 minutes. Carefully lift the baking dish from the water bath and allow to rest for 5 minutes for the sauce to settle.

Sift a little icing sugar over the top if you like, then serve at the table with whipped cream to pass around.

VARIATION: Add 25 g (1 oz/¼ cup) desiccated coconut to the batter, or use half lemon, half orange juice instead of lemon juice.

I wasn't around in the 1940s when this became really popular, but it is one of my favourite childhood desserts. I was always in the kitchen ready to help out with this recipe as it was easy enough for mum to hand it over for me to do the honours. For very little effort, this unique recipe produces a wonderful result — a light-as-air lemony sponge topping with a separate layer of sweet, creamy and slightly tangy sauce underneath. This dish is also known as lemon sponge pudding or lemon soufflé pudding in the UK and the US.

I'll admit I never tried golden syrup dumplings as a kid, but apparently most of my friends did. (What was going on at my house?) They are fabulous — a snap to make, with a surprisingly light texture — but you must eat them as soon as they are cooked or they'll become stodgy. Dollop on a blob of cream or ice cream and they're simply heaven on a cold night. A new-found friend, who'd have thought? Roll on winter...

✳ coconut & mandarin golden syrup dumplings

DUMPLINGS

125 g (4½ oz/1 cup) self-raising flour
60 g (2¼ oz) chilled unsalted butter, chopped
45 g (1¾ oz/½ cup) desiccated coconut, well toasted
1¼ teaspoons finely grated mandarin or lemon zest
1 large egg, lightly beaten
1 tablespoon milk

SYRUP

140 g (5 oz/¾ cup) soft brown sugar
260 g (9¼ oz/¾ cup) golden syrup (if unavailable,
   substitute with half honey & half dark corn syrup)
40 g (1½ oz) unsalted butter
80 ml (2½ fl oz/⅓ cup) strained, freshly squeezed
   mandarin juice
1½ tablespoons lemon juice
2 teaspoons mandarin liqueur, optional

makes 12 (serves 4–6)

To make the dumplings, sift the flour and a pinch of salt into a bowl, then rub the butter into the flour with your fingertips until the mixture resembles fine breadcrumbs. Stir in the coconut and mandarin zest. Add the combined egg and milk and mix to a soft dough using a flat-bladed knife. Set aside.

To make the syrup, put 500 ml (17 fl oz/2 cups) water in a deep-sided frying pan with the sugar, golden syrup, butter, mandarin juice and lemon juice. Stir over medium–high heat until the sugar has dissolved. Bring to the boil and cook for 3 minutes.

Meanwhile, working quickly, take 1 tablespoon of dumpling mixure at a time and shape into compact balls. You should end up with 12. Gently drop them into the syrup, then reduce to a simmer, cover and cook for 10 minutes, or until the tip of a small sharp knife comes out clean when inserted into the centre of a dumpling.

Spoon the dumplings into serving dishes. Stir the liqueur, if using, into the syrup, and ladle over the dumplings. Serve with fresh mandarin segments, sliced peaches or nectarines if you like, dolloped with some thick or whipped cream.

VARIATIONS: Add different spices such as cinnamon, nutmeg, saffron, ginger and cloves to the dumplings, and use finely chopped or ground nuts such as almonds, macadamias, pecans or hazelnuts (or a handful of grated raw apple) in place of the coconut.

✳ No wonder my dad used to love treacle tart — with such a perfectly tender crust and a balanced sweetness in the filling, the end result is simply delicious. Treacle has quite a strong molasses flavour, so feel free to replace it with golden syrup if you like. Other suggested substitutes are also given in the recipe below.

macadamia treacle tart

PASTRY

250 g (9 oz/2 cups) plain (all-purpose) flour
75 g (2¾ oz) unsalted butter, chilled & diced
75 g (2¾ oz) lard, chilled
55 g (2 oz/¼ cup) caster (superfine) sugar
1 egg, lightly beaten

FILLING

4 large eggs
¼ teaspoon lemon zest
1½ teaspoons lemon juice
1 teaspoon natural vanilla extract
½ teaspoon ground ginger, optional
260 g (9¼ oz/¾ cup) treacle or molasses
260 g (9¼ oz/¾ cup) golden syrup (if unavailable, substitute with half honey & half dark corn syrup)
250 ml (9 fl oz/1 cup) pouring (whipping) cream
80 g (2¾ oz/1 cup) fresh breadcrumbs
160 g (5¾ oz/1 cup) whole macadamia nuts, lightly toasted (see Note)

serves 8

To make the pastry, sift the flour and a pinch of salt into a large bowl. Grate the butter and lard over the top, then rub together with your fingertips until the mixture resembles breadcrumbs. Mix in the sugar. Add the egg and 3 teaspoons cold water and mix with a flat-bladed knife until the mixture clumps together. Gather into a ball, cover with plastic wrap and refrigerate for 30 minutes.

Preheat the oven to 180°C (350°F/Gas 4). Roll out the pastry between two sheets of baking paper or plastic wrap to a circle about 36 cm (14¼ inches) in diameter. Peel off the top layer and invert over a 24 cm (9½ inch) wide, 4 cm (1½ inch) deep, fluted, loose-based flan (tart) tin. Gently push the pastry into the edges of the tin, then trim the edges to 1 cm (½ inch) above the rim. Refrigerate for 20 minutes.

Loosely line the pastry with baking paper and fill with baking beads, uncooked rice or dried beans. Bake for 20 minutes, then remove the paper and weights and bake for a further 6–8 minutes, or until the edge of the pastry is pale golden and the base is dry to the touch. Remove from the oven and lower the oven temperature to 160°C (315°F/Gas 2–3).

While the pastry is blind-baking, make the filling. Put the eggs, lemon zest, lemon juice, vanilla and ginger, if using, into a bowl. Whisk until foamy, then mix in the treacle, golden syrup and cream until smooth. Add the breadcrumbs and macadamias and mix until thoroughly combined.

Pour the mixture into the pastry case and bake for 35–40 minutes, or until the filling is slightly puffed and dry to the touch — it should still be slightly wobbly, not set firm.

Remove the tart from the oven and allow to rest in the tin for 15 minutes, before transferring to a serving plate. Serve slices warm with ice cream, or a dollop of lightly whipped cream (spiked with rum, if you like).

NOTE: If you prefer, instead of the macadamia nuts you could use 160 g (5¾ oz/1 cup) blanched almonds or peanuts, or 100 g (3½ oz/1 cup) pecans or walnuts.

chocolate malted self-saucing pudding

60 g (2¼ oz) unsalted butter, chopped

300 ml (10½ fl oz) pouring (whipping) cream

300 g (10½ oz/2 cups) best-quality chopped dark chocolate

125 g (4½ oz/1 cup) self-raising flour

40 g (1½ oz/⅓ cup) good-quality unsweetened cocoa powder

50 g (1¾ oz/½ cup) malted milk powder

185 g (6½ oz/1 cup) soft brown sugar

2 large eggs, lightly beaten

½ teaspoon natural vanilla extract

icing (confectioners') sugar, to serve

serves 6–8

Preheat the oven to 180°C (350°F/Gas 4). Put the butter, cream and 200 g (7 oz/1⅓ cups) of the chocolate in a small saucepan and stir over medium–low heat until the chocolate has almost completely melted. Remove from the heat and stir until smooth.

Sift the flour, half the cocoa powder and half the malted milk powder into a bowl, then stir in half the sugar. Pour in the chocolate mixture and stir to combine. Add the egg and vanilla and combine thoroughly. Spoon one-third of the mixture into a greased 2.5-litre (87 fl oz/10 cup) non-metallic baking dish, about 7–8 cm (2¾–3¼ inches) deep. Evenly top with the remaining chocolate, then pour in the remaining pudding mixture and smooth over. Sift the remaining cocoa and malted milk powder, combine with the remaining sugar, then sprinkle evenly over the top of the pudding mixture. Place the baking dish in a roasting tin and pour in enough water to come halfway up the side of the baking dish.

Pour 310 ml (10¾ fl oz/1¼ cups) boiling water over the back of a spoon, over the entire surface of the pudding. (Using a spoon helps to more evenly and gently distribute the water so it doesn't form large dents or holes on top of the pudding.)

Bake for 55–60 minutes, or until the top of the pudding is firm and dry to the touch. Remove the pudding from the water bath and allow to rest for 5 minutes to let the sauce settle and thicken (be careful not to let the pudding rest much longer than this as it will absorb the sauce). Sift some icing sugar over the top and serve with a dollop of cream or ice cream, and perhaps some fresh strawberries, raspberries or pitted cherries.

I love chocolate self-saucing pudding — well, anything chocolate actually — but there's a real comfort in this dessert. Of course there's the incomparable aroma as it is pulled out of a hot oven, but it is the plunging of a spoon through the spongy topping through to the pool of fudgy chocolate sauce below that evokes a special childhood foodie memory for me. Here I have added some malt as for me, like most kids who grew up on the beaches, chocolate malted milkshakes were a dietary staple at the local milkbar, chocolate and malt being so very good together!

As the pavlova war rages I am uninclined to write anything about its dubious history — to be perfectly honest, I am not in the least bit concerned whether it is an Australian or New Zealand invention. Certainly, neither country was the first to combine meringue with cream and fruit, but that story is for another day ... However, one fact that no-one can dispute is that the humble pavlova tastes terrific — so much so that it is served at every sort of antipodean occasion, from a barbecue with the neighbours to Christmas Day.

✳ pavlova
with mango cream

MERINGUE

6 egg whites, at room temperature
1/2 teaspoon cream of tartar
345 g (12 oz/1 1/2 cups) caster (superfine) sugar
1 tablespoon cornflour (cornstarch)
1 1/2 teaspoons natural vanilla extract
1 1/2 teaspoons white vinegar

200 g (7 oz) ripe mango flesh (about 2 mangoes)
600 ml (21 fl oz) pouring (whipping) cream
your choice of ripe fruit, to decorate

serves 6–8

Preheat the oven to 180°C (350°F/Gas 4). To make the meringue, beat the egg whites and cream of tartar using electric beaters on high until soft peaks form. With the motor still running, very gradually add all the sugar. Combine the cornflour, vanilla and vinegar and stir until smooth, then beat into the meringue mixture. Continue beating for a further 10 minutes, or until the meringue peaks are stiff and glossy.

Draw a circle about 23 cm (9 inches) in diameter onto a piece of baking paper. Turn the paper over and line a large baking tray with it. Spoon the meringue into the centre of the circle, then evenly spread it out to the edge of the pencil line. Use the flat side of a spatula to smooth over the top, then make furrows around the outside edge of the meringue to make the edges stand up as straight as possible and higher than the centre, forming a natural hollow for the filling. This also helps to stop the edges cracking.

Place in the oven and immediately lower the temperature to 100°C (200°F/Gas 1/2). Bake for 1 hour 10 minutes. Turn off the oven but leave the pavlova in the oven to cool completely, with the door propped slightly ajar with a wooden spoon.

Meanwhile, finely dice the mango flesh. Whip the cream in a bowl until it holds firm peaks. Gently fold the mango through the cream until well combined, but be careful not to beat out the air. Refrigerate until ready to serve. Whisk again just before serving to thicken, if necessary.

Spoon the mango cream into the pavlova hollow and spread over the top of the pavlova with the back of the spoon. Arrange a selection of fruit decoratively on top and serve.

VARIATION: If mango is not in season, mix 210 g (7 1/2 oz/2/3 cup) of pineapple conserve through the cream instead — delicious!

Bread and butter puddings, both sweet and savoury, were developed as a thrifty way to use up stale bread — sounds appetizing, huh? Additionally, due to its soft texture, it was often served as 'invalid' food. Well get me to the nearest bed! A good English-style bread and butter pudding can be one of the most satisfying yet simple desserts around — especially when it's dished up with a dollop of cream or a luxurious scoop of vanilla bean ice cream.

bread & butter pudding

350 g (12 oz) day-old brioche or loaf of bread
80 g (2¾ oz) unsalted butter, softened
6 egg yolks
80 g (2¾ oz/⅓ cup) caster (superfine) sugar
45 g (1¾ oz/¼ cup) soft brown sugar
250 ml (9 fl oz/1 cup) milk
500 ml (17 fl oz/2 cups) pouring (whipping) cream
1 teaspoon natural vanilla extract

½ teaspoon ground cinnamon
1 tablespoon caster (superfine) sugar, extra

serves 6–8

Thickly slice the brioche and spread each side with the softened butter. Use any leftover butter to grease a non-metallic 1.5–2 litre (52–70 fl oz/6–8-cup capacity) baking dish measuring about 6 cm (2½ inches) deep. Cut the brioche slices into 4 cm (1½ inch) squares and place in the prepared dish.

Preheat the oven to 160°C (315°F/Gas 2–3). Put the egg yolks, caster sugar, brown sugar, milk, cream and vanilla in a bowl and whisk until smooth. Pour the mixture over the brioche, then press the brioche down into the custard. Leave for 20 minutes to ensure the brioche really soaks up the custard.

Combine the cinnamon and extra caster sugar and sprinkle evenly over the pudding. Bake for 50 minutes, or until puffed and golden. Serve warm with whipped cream or ice cream, and perhaps some poached fruit.

VARIATIONS: You could bake the pudding in individual serving dishes, which will reduce the cooking time. Also, try adding a handful of one of the following: raisins, dried cherries, cranberries, chopped dried fruit (apricots, dates, figs), slivered or flaked nuts, chopped chocolate or toasted desiccated coconut. You can also experiment with your favourite breads, such as wholemeal (whole-wheat), raisin or walnut bread — or go all out with chocolate croissants or leftover banana or coconut bread!

baked banana cheesecake

BASE

150 g (5½ oz) digestive biscuits (cookies)
100 g (3½ oz/heaped ¾ cup) very finely chopped
    walnuts, macadamia nuts or pecans
½ teaspoon ground ginger
100 g (3½ oz) unsalted butter, melted

FILLING

625 g (1 lb 6 oz/2½ cups) cream cheese, softened
145 g (5½ oz/⅔ cup) caster sugar
2 large ripe bananas, mashed until very smooth
3 large eggs
4 large egg yolks
1 teaspoon very finely grated lime zest
1½ tablespoons lime juice
2 teaspoons vanilla extract

TOPPING

300 ml (10½ fl oz) sour cream
1 tablespoon honey
2–3 tablespoons pouring (whipping) cream
pulp from 2 panama passionfruit

serves 8–10

Break the biscuits into small pieces, then process in a food processor or blender until crumb-like. Add the nuts, ginger and melted butter and process until well combined.

Invert the base of a 23 cm (9 inch) diameter, 7 cm (2¾ inch) deep, non-stick spring-form cake tin so the rim is facing down — this makes for a firmer fit, which prevents any water from the waterbath seeping into the tin (which makes a soggy cheesecake). Evenly press the crumbs into the base of the spring-form tin and refrigerate until ready to use.

Preheat the oven to 150°C (300°F/Gas 2). To make the filling, beat the cream cheese using electric beaters for 10–12 minutes, or until absolutely smooth. Really check for any little lumps and keep beating until you are sure they are all gone — this will ensure the silkiest, creamiest texture. Add the sugar and mashed banana and beat again until smooth. Lightly beat the eggs and egg yolks together, then add to the mixture and beat again until incorporated and smooth. Mix in the lime zest, lime juice and vanilla until well combined.

Wrap the base of the spring-form tin tightly with plastic wrap (the water bath will not be hot enough to melt the plastic wrap), then take a few long sheets of extra-wide foil and firmly wrap it around the base and sides, to prevent water seepage. Pour the filling into the prepared tin and tap the base on a bench to release any air bubbles. Prick any visible bubbles with a small skewer.

Sit the cheesecake in a roasting tin and pour in enough boiling water to come halfway up the side of the spring-form tin. Bake for 1 hour 10 minutes, or until the filling is just set, but still slightly wobbly and dry to the touch.

To make the topping, whisk together the sour cream and honey with just enough cream to produce a smooth, easily spreadable, thick liquid consistency. Carefully spoon the topping over the cheesecake, smoothing it over. Bake for a further 10 minutes, or until the sour cream in the topping has just set. The topping will appear quite glossy, but will firm up further on resting and chilling.

Carefully remove the cheesecake from the waterbath, snip off the foil and discard. Allow to cool in the tin, on a wire rack, to room temperature, then cover and refrigerate overnight. This is important for the final setting process and texture.

When ready to serve, run a hot knife between the spring-form tin and the cheesecake, then remove the cheesecake from the tin. Serve sliced, with a little passionfruit pulp drizzled over the top.

Visitors to Australia are often bemused by larger-than-life statues such as the Big Pineapple and the Big Prawn that mark several regional towns. I think it was too many road trips past the iconic Big Banana on the northern coast of New South Wales that may have turned me off eating bananas raw — but if bananas always came in cheesecake form I would grow fur and a long tail and move into a zoo! This heavenly baked cheesecake is enough to bring out the monkey in all of us.

✳ *Dating back to the 1500s and originally served warm, the trifle's history is as rich as its contents: custard, cake, fruit, cream and sometimes jelly! A well-balanced meal if you ask me, and quaintly referred to by some as a 'charming confusion' — a fitting description if ever I heard one. I am not suggesting you dig out your grandmother's best cut-glass bowl, but do make sure you serve this, as is traditional, in a glass bowl, so you can see all the lovely layers.*

trifle

STRAWBERRY JELLY

500 g (1 lb 2 oz/3⅓ cups) very ripe strawberries
230 g (8½ oz/1 cup) caster (superfine) sugar
15 g (½ oz/1½ sachets) powdered gelatine
1 tablespoon strawberry liqueur

VANILLA CUSTARD

500 ml (17 fl oz/2 cups) milk
500 ml (17 fl oz/2 cups) pouring (whipping) cream
1 vanilla bean, split lengthways & seeds scraped
6 egg yolks
80 g (2¾ oz/⅓ cup) caster (superfine) sugar

1 single day-old sponge cake (200 g/7 oz)
   (either from page 112 or store-bought)
125 ml (4 fl oz/½ cup) sweet sherry or dessert wine
250 g (9 oz/1⅔ cups) strawberries, sliced, plus extra
   sliced strawberries, to decorate
300 ml (10½ fl oz) pouring (whipping) cream,
   lightly whipped

serves 6–8

To make the strawberry jelly, hull the strawberries and process in a blender or food processor until smooth. Place in a saucepan with the sugar and 500 ml (17 fl oz/2 cups) water and stir over high heat until the sugar has dissolved. Strain into a clean pan. Pour 60 ml (2 fl oz/¼ cup) of the hot liquid into a small bowl and sprinkle the gelatine over the top. Wait until it becomes spongy, then whisk until smooth with a fork. Pour it back into the pan and stir over medium–high heat until the gelatine has completely dissolved. Pour into a shallow dish and stir in the liqueur. Allow to cool slightly, then cover and refrigerate for 4 hours, or until set. Roughly chop or dice the jelly just before assembling the trifle.

While the jelly is setting, make the vanilla custard. Put the milk, cream, and vanilla bean and seeds in a saucepan over medium–high heat. Bring just to the boil, then remove from the heat, cover and allow to infuse for 15 minutes. Whisk together the egg yolks and sugar until thick and smooth. Gradually whisk the warm milk mixture into the eggs until smooth, then return the mixture to the pan. Put the pan back over medium–low heat and stir constantly for 10–12 minutes, or until the custard has thickened and easily coats the back of a spoon. Allow to cool to room temperature.

Cut the cake into 2 cm (¾ inch) cubes and line the base of a very deep glass bowl with half the cubes. Sprinkle half the sherry over the sponge. Scatter half the sliced strawberries over the top, then top with half the custard and half the chopped jelly. Repeat with a layer of sponge, sherry, sliced strawberries, custard and jelly. Spoon the whipped cream over to cover the top. Cover with plastic wrap and refrigerate for at least 6 hours, or overnight. Before serving, decorate with the extra sliced strawberries.

VARIATIONS: Trifles can be made with almost any leftover un-iced (un-frosted) cake — the trick is to match the other flavours. For example, if you wanted to use chocolate cake, you could combine it with, say, coffee jelly, coffee liqueur and bananas. Or use orange cake with orange jelly and sliced peaches. Or coconut cake with sliced mango and passionfruit jelly — the possibilities are endless.

When we were kids my parents used to take us to the local drive-in cinema for a fun family outing. We took blankets and pillows and made ourselves very comfy, but one of the most special parts of the evening for me was the quick stop on the way to pick up piping-hot banana and pineapple fritters to munch on through the movie. The caramel rum sauce is an optional feature and rated Adults Only.

*banana fritters
with caramel rum sauce

CARAMEL RUM SAUCE
230 g (8$^{1}/_{2}$ oz/1 cup) caster (superfine) sugar
125 ml (4 fl oz/$^{1}/_{2}$ cup) pouring (whipping) cream
1 tablespoon rum
1 teaspoon natural vanilla extract

125 g (4$^{1}/_{2}$ oz/1 cup) plain (all-purpose) flour
310 ml (10$^{3}/_{4}$ fl oz/1$^{1}/_{4}$ cups) beer
vegetable oil, for deep-frying
4 large ripe (but not mushy) bananas
ice cream, to serve

serves 6

To make the caramel rum sauce, put the sugar and 125 ml (4 fl oz/ $^{1}/_{2}$ cup) water in a saucepan and stir over medium–high heat until the sugar has dissolved. When the mixture comes to the boil, cook for 20 minutes without stirring until the sugar is dark golden — swirl the pan a few times during cooking to ensure it caramelizes evenly. Take the pan off the heat and carefully pour in the cream, rum and vanilla. Take care as the mixture will bubble up, but it will settle. Put the pan back on the heat and stir until smooth. Cook for 2 minutes, or until thickened, then turn off the heat.

Combine the flour and beer, whisking until smooth. Allow to rest for 15 minutes, then whisk again.

While the batter is resting, fill a deep-fryer or large heavy-based saucepan one-third full of oil and heat to 180°C (350°F), or until a cube of bread dropped into the oil browns in 15 seconds.

Peel the bananas and cut into slices 1.5 cm ($^{5}/_{8}$ inch) thick. Dip the banana slices in the batter, allowing any excess to drip back into the bowl. Deep-fry in batches for 4–5 minutes, or until golden and crisp. Drain well on paper towels.

Serve drizzled with the warm caramel rum sauce, with a scoop of vanilla bean or macadamia ice cream.

One of those sweet, comforting desserts that made a clean sweep through restaurants and cafés during the 1980s and 90s: if it wasn't on the menu there would be hell to pay — until we almost overdosed on it, that is. These days it is more often cooked at home for a special family dinner — it seems we all still love a good one, even if it has slipped out of fashion. This version is moist and flavoursome with plenty of sauce, so you can pour over as much or as little as you like. Go on, try it one more time.

sticky date pudding

350 g (12 oz/2 cups) pitted fresh dates, chopped
1½ teaspoons ground ginger
1 teaspoon ground cinnamon
½ teaspoon bicarbonate of soda (baking soda)
150 g (5½ oz) unsalted butter, softened & chopped
95 g (3½ oz/½ cup) soft brown sugar
90 g (3¼ oz/¼ cup) golden syrup (if unavailable,
   substitute with half honey & half dark corn syrup)
2 large eggs
185 g (6½ oz/1½ cups) self-raising flour, sifted

SAUCE
375 ml (13 fl oz/1½ cups) pouring (whipping) cream
45 g (1¾ oz/¼ cup) soft brown sugar
40 g (1½ oz) unsalted butter
1 teaspoon natural vanilla extract

serves 8–10

Preheat the oven to 180°C (350°F/Gas 4). Grease and line the base of a deep, 20 cm (8 inch) square, non-stick cake tin.

Put the dates, ginger, cinnamon and bicarbonate of soda in a heatproof bowl and pour in 310 ml (10¾ fl oz/1¼ cups) boiling water. Stir and leave to absorb for about 15 minutes.

Beat the butter, sugar and golden syrup using electric beaters until pale and creamy. Beat in the eggs, one at a time, until well incorporated. Mix in the flour until smooth, then add the date mixture, mixing thoroughly. Pour into the prepared tin and bake for 50 minutes, or until a skewer inserted into the centre of the pudding comes out clean. Remove from the oven, allow to cool slightly in the tin, then invert onto a serving platter.

Meanwhile, make the sauce. Put the cream, sugar, butter and vanilla in a saucepan and stir with a metal spoon over medium–high heat until the sugar has dissolved. Bring to the boil, then reduce the heat and simmer for 20 minutes, or until thickened and glossy.

Cut the cake into serving portions. Serve drizzled with a little sauce, with extra sauce in a jug for people to help themselves. Lovely with whipped cream or vanilla bean ice cream.

NOTE: If you have to make this pudding ahead of time, top a slice with some sauce and heat briefly in a microwave before serving.

index